Telling Truth

The Foolishness of Preaching

in a Real World

030454
8

7 —

Telling Truth

The Foolishness of Preaching

in a Real World

James Armstrong

WORD BOOKS, PUBLISHER

WACO, TEXAS

In gratitude for the incomparable ministries
of
Frederick W. Robertson
Phillips Brooks
Harry Emerson Fosdick

Contents

True Christian preaching is . . . a proclamation which claims to be the call of God through the mouth of [humans] and, as the word of authority, demands belief. It is its characteristic paradox that in it we meet God's call in human words.

—Rudolf Bultmann

It pleased God by the foolishness of preaching to save them that believe.

—Paul

Chapters 2–5 were first delivered, in an earlier and abbreviated form, as the Voigt Lectures at McKendree College in Lebanon, Illinois. They were also shared with The United Methodist Pastors' School of the Dakotas Area in 1975. A brief section of chapter one first appeared in the Introduction to *The Urgent Now*.

Chapter One

Chapter One

Truth-Telling in a Real World

Preaching is truth-telling. Truth-telling is based upon reality. And reality—now as always—is hard to grasp and harder still to rightly interpret. This is especially true if those who listen to the preacher are confined to narrow, insulated worlds.

At Temple University not long ago a small band of academicians and religious leaders shared a day-long conversation based on a perceptive position paper by the ethicist, John Curtis Raines. The paper and the conversation were designed to deal with the fundamental issues intruding upon the mood and milieu of America's dominant middle class, and with the middle class' ability to understand, absorb, and morally respond to the challenges the issues posed.

We talked about taxes and tax reform; affluence and consumerism; unemployment and inflation; bureaucratic boondoggling and thrift in government; health, education and politics; Third World reality and angry impatience pressing in upon the self-protected worlds most of us inhabit. An engaging young economist began and ended the day with the comment, "I'm gloomy." As points were made through the course of the day he would punctuate the discussion with the same phrase: "I'm gloomy." There was nothing superficial about his verbal shrug. He was not trying to be flippant or facetious. He *was* gloomy—and for the best of reasons. In the light of available data, overriding impressions and values shared, there seemed to be few signs of hope on the horizons of political probability and distributive justice. The few rich would continue to get richer, the masses of the poor would continue to multiply and get poorer and those caught in the middle—the middle class of the United States—would unwittingly foot the bill and naïvely identify with the process and claim it as their own.

Robert Heilbroner's *Inquiry into the Human Prospect* was the epitome of pessimism. It talked about the failure of nerve of the American people. Vietnam taught us that we are not all-powerful, all-knowing, and always right. The upsurge of violence everywhere around us intimidates and frightens us. Political assassinations and kidnappings, terrorist bombings, the hijacking of airplanes, widespread murder in the name of ideological objectives, and, in our nearer, everyday worlds, the soaring statistics of violent crime—this blatant barbarism is jarring us from the complacency of our middle-class isolation and reminding us that personal safety is no longer a security to be taken for granted. Heilbroner wrote about changing values and life-styles, drugs, sexual promiscuity, and the rejection of traditional attitudes toward responsibility;

about the "betrayal" of norms most of us have long taken for granted.

His overview of world conditions was equally bleak. He is convinced that unless advanced nations cut back on their technological and industrial development, unless ways are created for the dramatic redistribution of the world's wealth, unless the loyalties and life-styles of the affluent are transformed, there is virtually no hope for the survival of the human race.

Heilbroner and Raines assume that the hope of humanity's survival, bleak as it is, is somehow linked with the western world. Not so—necessarily—says L. S. Stavrianos. His *Promise of the Coming Dark Age* accentuates the *promise*. He argues that Marxism is a major new world religion, suggesting that our preoccupation with western technology, productivity, and competitiveness has blinded us to the near miraculous phenomena of China. Hunger, long the plague of China, is now more prevalent in Appalachia than in China. Unemployment, long the plague of China, is now more endemic in the capitalist nations of the West than in China. He quotes Jacob Bronowski from *The Ascent of Man:*

> The ascent of man will go on. But do not assume that it will go on by Western civilization as we know it. We are being weighed in the balance at this moment. If we give up, the next step will be taken—but not by us. . . . If we do not take the next step in the ascent of man, it will be taken by people elsewhere, in Africa and China.

There are whisperings of promise and hope, even amidst the travail of the apparent collapse of western values and aspirations. The Christian, grateful for and responsive to these, looks beyond the promise of the earthbound.

A theology of hope is, by definition, theological. It may deal with politics and culture but it is basically religious. Is it possible for "mainline" churches, middle class in orientation and makeup, to honestly, aggressively, and redemptively deal with the issues Raines and Heilbroner raise? Or, are we trapped by our own folkways and pocketbook biases? In his 1975 Christmas message Pope Paul VI pleaded for the nonviolent liberation of people living in impoverished nations. Speaking on their behalf he commended those who are "engaged with all their energy in the effort and struggle to overcome everything which condemns (the poor and powerless) to remain on the margin of life: famine, chronic disease, illiteracy, poverty, injustice in international relations and especially in commercial exchange situations of economic and cultural neocolonialism sometimes as cruel as the old political colonialism." He said the Roman Catholic Church has the duty of "assisting the birth of this liberation, giving witness to it, of ensuring that it is complete." How does one interpret this mission to people who are threatened by it and predisposed to fight it on the basis of cultural preconditioning? How does the truth-teller convince his or her hearers that such questions are fundamentally religious; theological?

Richard Neuhaus in his evaluation of the American experiment, *Time Toward Home*, takes much of the Raines/Heilbroner thesis for granted. He deplores declining morality, economic injustice, senseless wars, world hunger and the self-idolatry of nations. But, he also talks about God's covenant with his people, "destination ethics", and the role of the church. Assuming the absolute seriousness of history, Neuhaus writes: "Christians are those who have been alerted in advance to the meaning of universal history, and their mission is to alert the world to its destiny." We have been placed here in this imperfect time to *alert* the world, to proclaim the Word, to verbalize and demonstrate forms of saving truth.

Denominational emphases and programs with their study and action resources have central roles to play in all of this.

The development of informed, balanced, outspoken educational materials to be used on a continuing basis by the various age levels of local churches is even more important. That which liberation theologians call "conscientization" must become a part of the experience of parish life.

The use of religious periodicals (most of these are struggling for their very existence today) is indispensable, as is the introduction of congregations to secular, issue-oriented newspapers, magazines, and other publications that inform minds and stimulate community action and political involvement.

The creation and imaginative employment of task forces, action groups and missional outreach tools to deal with specific domestic and overseas needs must be a part of this process.

But, what of the pulpit? Does the sermon as an integral part of the worship experience of a gathered congregation have a significant role to play in days like these? Does it have a legitimate interpretive, prodding, truth-telling function? Or does it represent mere "foolishness," not in Pauline terms but as a matter of fact?

A headline appearing in a midwestern newspaper some years ago captured the cynicism and faddism of the time: "Espresso Priest Says Sermon Is Obsolete." The clergyman who was pronouncing last rites over the sermon found his particular niche in writing plays and holding forth on an elevated stool under a spotlight in coffee houses and nightclubs. (Power to his kind as long as they don't judge others who share neither their skills nor exclusive—sometimes elitist—commitments.) Obviously, the gifted priest had given up on "the art of preaching." There are droves of clergy who see little if any linkage between the world as it is and the pulpit's mandate to alert the world. This shrug in the face of homiletics started long ago. In the 1920's seminaries began to deemphasize preaching. They featured an assortment of sometimes new, usually valid, always compelling curricula themes; "waves of the future" they sometimes argued: Christian education, social action, pastoral counseling, small groups, a variety of renewal patterns and thrusts, community organization, political involvement, participation in "the Movement" and alternate life-styles—all valuable contributions to the church's understanding of its mission, but not the new messiahs some fancied them to be. In the process worship and preaching were indulged as concessions to a worn-out past or confused with bouncing balls, floating balloons, and tentative dialogue.* The implications were clear. Sermons had "had their day and ceased to be."

In 1969, *The Pulpit*, the prestigious "journal of contemporary preaching" was put to rest after forty years of distinguished service. It was replaced by a magazine that stated: "The mission of the Church requires a new style with new skills for its fulfillment." What did that mean?

---

*Worship *is* celebration. It can be dramatically innovative and marvelously, redemptively creative. But strobe lights, multi-media presentations and psychedelic impressions have not yet supplanted Bach, Handel, and two thousand years of valued liturgical experience. And, authentic preaching (including conversational and dialogical techniques) will remain vital to the experience of gathered Christians.

Traditionally verbal proclamation had been a basic ingredient in the life of the church. Even now, in spite of decades of neglect, few would call for its abandonment. But its role has been under serious review. In his swan song the editor of *The Pulpit*, preparing for the successor journal, wrote, "We do not intend to minimize preaching; we intend to give this indispensable and demanding task its proper setting by seeing it in relation to the total task of the church's mission." No longer was preaching seen as an end in itself. It was—as it should be—viewed in context against the backdrop of the church's total ministry.

Two things seem obvious:

1. There are no more "pulpit giants." True, world-famous evangelists, utilizing electronic miracles and public relations expertise, have preached to more people than any other preachers in the history of Christendom. But their preaching—compelling as it may be—has little in common with the theological balance, ethical sensitivity, and intellectual discipline of the masters of the past. Then too, there are the "pulpit personalities" who preach to standing-room-only crowds with their self-help schemes and "rah-rah" words. But, their sermons are hardly the sermons of a Buttrick or a Tittle. They are more like weathervanes, responding to the cultural neuroses and reflecting the self-centered preoccupations of an entrenched and affluent society. We have much to learn from such effective communicators, but if they become our models, our ministries will lack balance and wholeness.

2. Much preaching is unrelated to forms of reality most people are called upon to cope with. That is the thing to be said for the preaching of a Billy Graham or a Norman Vincent Peale. Sometimes their words seem to provide escape from certain forms of reality. But they have recognized and addressed some of the universal themes of

human existence: sin, anxiety, illness, brokenness, and powerlessness. Frankly, that is more than many of their most vocal critics have done. Yet, authentic biblical preaching can never be limited to individualized salvation, privatized morality, and providing balm in Gilead.

The outgoing editor of *The Pulpit* was absolutely right when he saw preaching "in relation to the total task of the church's mission." Statistically, in terms of numbers preached to and dollars given, preaching in context may seem less effective than catering to popular demand. But the Christian minister is called to be more concerned about *truth-telling* and *faithfulness to the biblical witness* than about adaptation to prevailing winds of vested interest and cultural or religious faddism. The questions remain: Does the sermon have a valid function in disordered days like these? Can it communicate truth and interpret hard-to-accept dimensions of reality to people who are bogged down in quagmires of disillusionment, anger, materialistic self-centeredness, and personal defeat?

Contextual preaching must be seen as more than a benign clergy offering verbal sweets or an impatient voice thundering judgments from the pulpit. It will deal with life as it is in the light of biblical truth. In 1965 Watts was the scene of one of this century's most tragic and bloody riots. Some time later I was asked to preach the ordination sermon of one of my former students who had been called to direct the urban ministries of the Disciples of Christ in Los Angeles. The service was held in the United Christian Church of Watts just a few blocks from infamous Charcoal Alley. Most of the people present were black. The procession was led by two young black women wearing African dress and carrying crosses. Their hair was natural; their bearing proud. The music—a far cry from Fannie Crosby —was provided by a folk-and-rock combo called Kind.

The congregational hymns were "Blowin' in the Wind," "Let's Get Together," and "He was a Friend of Mine" (an ode bemoaning the deaths of John F. Kennedy and Martin Luther King, Jr.). Representatives of many denominations, government offices, and secular agencies were present and participating. Although an outsider, I joined in the "laying on of hands." After the benediction the combo picked up the beat, a mini-skirted vocalist began to sing and demonstrative youngsters danced around the chancel as their elders mingled, chatted, and reflected on the events of the night.

I had preached—about conflict and reconciliation, priorities and peace; about a living Christ at work amidst the violent madness of today's world. When it was over a young fellow in a leather jacket self-consciously sidled up to me and said, "You have 'soul', man." I hope so. But bear in mind, in that context the sermon was part of a total experience, an experience based upon painful recent memory, an experience reaching out beyond the walls and creeds of an institution into the struggles and dreams of a people.

Raines and Heilbroner present grim pictures of present reality. Later we will refer to the Irish playwright, George Bernard Shaw, who considered himself a "preacher" without a message. World War II had shot all sense of certainty "out of (his) hands". Preaching today dare not disregard the insane madness of the contemporary scene. It must take into account the brokenness, anger, and confusion of masses of people. But it must also express and verbalize the particular truths and values of Christianity in relationship to other forms of truth and conflicting values. The sermon must somehow be liberated from the hackneyed phrases, tired jargon, and simplistic notions that undisciplined and uninformed clergy too often and too easily rely on. Inflation, unemployment, racism, sexism, Third World suffering, and other forms of geopolitical reality may seem far removed from old First Church, but unless First Church's pulpit is aware of their implications it will fail to inform and guide its present constituency or command the respect of critical outsiders who have little regard for the church as they see it and its message as they hear it.

Phillips Brooks, in many respects the most influential preacher the United States has produced, was only forty-two when he delivered his Yale lectures on preaching. Those lectures have provided much of the stimulus for this book. Seventy-five years ago the scholar, T. Harwood Pattison, wrote, "[Brooks'] mission as a preacher seemed to be to render theology into life. Truth in the abstract . . . had little charm for him." The truth-telling of the Christian, while transcendent in its points of reference, must be down-to-earth. It must face real pepole in a real world, addressing the deepest individual needs of those people while probing and interpreting the demanding complexities and mandates for radical change that are integral to the present scene. Such preaching will save us from what Richard Neuhaus calls "resignation to the cave and loss of nerve in the face of the future."

Chapter Two

Chapter Two

Learning Truth

Charles Edward Jefferson, a renowned preacher of an earlier generation, said, "The minister is a prophet of the Lord. . . . He is a truth-teller, and therefore, first of all, must be a truth-seeker." That is what this chapter is all about: seeking forms of truth.

The early Phillips Brooks' contribution to the Lyman Beecher Lectures on Preaching still stands as the classic of the series. In it, the Boston cleric offered his famous definition of preaching. "Preaching," he said, "is the bringing of truth through personality." But—what is truth?

Two plus two equals four is a *fact*.

Sulphuric acid consists of two parts hydrogen, one part sulphur, and four parts oxygen. That's a *fact*.

Indians discovered America long before Columbus did. That's a *fact*. But factual knowledge only skips along the surface of truth.

While exploring different approaches to truth I went to my bookshelves and pulled down some old college texts on logic and philosophy. There were sections in these neglected tomes on instinct, custom, tradition, consensus, feeling, sense, intuition, consequences and coherence; on intellectualism, anti-conceptualism, and pragmatism. But those sterile avenues proved as musty and remote as a Victorian closet.

One supposedly discredited definition of truth in one of those books was this: "Truth is reality." Discredited or not, it is a starting point. If you push out the boundaries on that one, if your concept of reality is broad enough, deep enough, personal enough, truths will begin to come into focus.

A young mother who has miscarried one child and lost another sits on her sunporch, rocks gently back and forth and breastfeeds her little boy, a newborn baby who has been born healthy and is very much alive. The gift and the love and the promise are undeniable. That's reality.

You share a brilliant sunset with your beloved, looking at the stark configuration of limbs and branches, of winter trees silhouetted against the dull but glowing crimson of a fading sky. You reach out, touch fingertips and rejoice in the wonder of creation. That beauty and that love are real.

However, reality is not limited to the intimate and subjective. Adlai Stevenson was one of the most underrated public figures of this century. Twice defeated as a presidential candidate, accused of being indecisive, derisively referred to as an "egghead," he courageously fought the cheap and phony patriotism of "McCarthyism," championed and reflected the politics of high-mindedness, and, as our ambassador to the United Nations, was universally respected as an architect of global idealism. Today, more than a decade after his untimely death in London, his speeches read as warm and penetrating models of responsible communication. When he died the *New York Times* editorialized:

> Stevenson knew defeat and disappointment, but he never knew vulgarity, panic or despair. He was no stranger to ambition, but he remembered that, win or lose, he had to live with himself. . . . To the public dialogue of his time he brought intelligence, civility, and grace. We who have been his contemporaries have been companions of greatness.

The ambivalence and heartbreak, the loneliness, satisfaction and accomplishments of public life and leadership—they are real, too.

Truth and reality are one. God, who is ultimate reality, is, in the lexicon of the Christian faith, love. That is truth. That is real. Ultimate reality, the Word, "became flesh and lived among us . . . full of grace and truth." A vacillating Pilate, in his curious anguish, asked, "What is truth?" Jesus said, "I am the . . . truth." But, the Son of man did not limit the meaning of truth to divine reality, either abstract or incarnate. He said, "If *you* live within the revelation I have brought . . . *you* shall know the truth, and the truth will set you free."

It is our purpose here to consider the communication, the sharing of truth. That truth embraces love and grace, beauty and hope, private dreams and public deeds; persons both obscure and famous; the rich humanity of forgiveness, compassion, striving and fulfillment; a grasp of history, a knowledge of contemporary reality and an informed vision of future possibility. It is, at once, human and divine. But if such truth is to be shared it must first be appropriated. How can we learn the truth as we are called upon to communicate?

Learning is a mysterious and profound process. No cheap shortcuts lead into its presence. *Discipline, sheer uncompromising intellectual discipline, is a requisite in claiming the sorts and varieties of truth that can help refashion persons and recreate a bewildered, threatened world.*

I am not sure why some of our ministries grow so unsatisfying and ineffective. We have the freedom to do with our time what we will. Maybe we become so busy (and we can be ridiculously busy) with nonessentials, that we bypass the nurturing basics of authentic ministry. We don't reflect and meditate; we don't pray; we don't study; we don't do the *work* we are called to do. Maybe we are distracted by claims on our time that come from persons or activities that take us away from our sacred vocation. Or maybe we don't know how to handle our freedom and grow sluggish and lazy. Probably sloth, as much as anything else, reduces ministry to levels of mediocrity and relative impotence. Sloth, indolence, a refusal to pay the disciplined price of effective servanthood, rob countless clergy across this land of fulfilling their individual potential.

C. E. Jefferson once said, "An ignorant pulpit is the worst of all scourges." If our pulpit is uninformed and unenlightened we have no one to blame but ourselves. Some years ago a librarian conducted a clergy survey, the results of which were reported in the *New York Times.* The writer, with a measure of smug satisfaction, said:

> The reading habits of clergymen are slovenly, without plan or discipline, and fall short of the standard one would expect of a group with such high educational background and so rich an opportunity for intellectual leadership.

Because of my present responsibilities I find myself in

more ministers' studies today than ever before. My curiosity almost always leads me to their bookshelves. As often as not the results are disappointing; sometimes they are downright disheartening. One lifts the books and blows the dust away. The dates of publication may screech to a sudden halt with the last year the pastor spent in college or seminary. (There is wasteful sadness present when the most recent book on "salvation" owned by a fifty-year-old preacher is Knudson's *Doctrine of Redemption,* circa 1933; and his most recent foray into ethics is Niebuhr's *Moral Man and Immoral Society* of the same vintage.) Then there are those libraries that boast little more than books of jokes and illustrations, homiletical crutches and sermon "helps." There are libraries that reflect the narrow gauge and limited perspective of the owner; no breadth of range, no depth of scholarship, only the confirmation of limited tastes and prejudices cultivated years and years before. A seminary professor of mine once told of a young man who wrote a book at the age of twenty-six and spent the rest of his life defending it. Some of our bookshelves look like that. They give little indication of growth and development; of a reaching out that speaks of an expanding mind, an awareness of a harsh and brutal world or of a spirit that defies rational boundaries.

You may have seen the lines:

> Your little hands,
> Your little feet,
> Your little mouth,
> O God, how sweet.
>
> Your little nose,
> Your little ears,
> Your eyes that shed
> Such little tears.

> Your little voice,
> So soft, so kind;
> *Your little soul.*
> *Your little mind.*

Such littleness of spirit denies the possibility of effective servant ministry, yet it spells out the emotional and intellectual straitjackets in which many of us function. Apart from disciplined growth there can be no adequate preparation for truth-telling.

If such discipline is part of learning the truth, where do we begin? With the source book of our faith—*the Bible.* Not only is the laity riddled through with debilitating forms of biblical illiteracy; so, too, is the clergy. Our knowledge of the Bible needs to be a good deal more than the Sunday school youngster's ability to reel off the names of the sixty-six books; more than the literalist's ability to quote chapter and verse, ad infinitum, ad nauseam; more than the latest theories *about* the Bible. We need to experience the *reality* of the Scriptures; live and breathe the *truth* of the Scriptures.

Albert Outler, in his stimulating little book, *Theology in the Wesleyan Spirit,* says, "Wesley *lived* the Scriptures. [That's what I mean.] . . . his mind ranged over the Bible's length and breadth and depth like a radar, tuned into the pertinent data on every point he cared to make."

Wesley once wrote a friend saying he had come to a point where he was studying "no book but the Bible." (Incidentally, he wrote that eight years *before* Aldersgate.) In 1746 he wrote that he intended to be "a man of just one book." But when he talked about his loyalty to "Scripture alone" he never meant "nothing but Scripture." One scholar, dissecting his sermons, discovered that he quoted Horace, Virgil, Ovid, Cicero, Plato, Aristotle,

Augustine, and Kempis. He knew the medieval mystics and the Renaissance secularists, patristic theology and the Reformation classics. He quoted freely from Shakespeare and Milton. If we are Wesleyan in spirit, as many who read these words profess to be, we will study history and science, even as he did. We will cultivate an intimate awareness of the culture of which we are a part. But, we will also be biblical persons. As Albert Outler suggests, "Scripture was [Wesley's] first and final norm for the validation of any theological discussion. This meant a lifelong, total immersion in Scripture . . . in its dominant themes and images, in all its parts and in its organic wholeness."

Alexander Maclaren, called "the prince of the expositors," died as an old man in 1910. He was still in his teens when asked to supply Portsmouth Chapel in Southampton. It was, he was told, a "temporary" arrangement, but he refused all social engagements, arose at daybreak, and studied until late at night. His diligence paid off. He was called to be the pastor of the church. Later he would say any sermon worth hearing required sixty hours of labor a week.

When thirty-two years old Maclaren went to Union Chapel in Manchester where he stayed for fifty-two years. Every day, for sixty-eight years, he read the Bible in its original languages. Preaching to two thousand people each Sunday, he bound himself to the most demanding habits of study, wrote his sermons out in longhand, and left his *Exposition of the Holy Scriptures* and his contributions to the *Expositor's Bible* behind. (His commentary on the Psalms remains something of a classic to this day.) Ministry is much more than preaching; study is much more than "Bible study"; and, anyone who spends sixty hours a week on a sermon is a misguided fool. That weekly regimen would suggest priorities askew and a total ignorance of the context of authentic ministry today. But, before brushing Maclaren aside, let me ask a series of questions:

How much disciplined time do you spend with your Bible each week? Over the past year, how many hours have you devoted to searching out the riches of the Old Covenant—the stern insights of its Law, the judgments of its prophets, the holy awareness of its poets, the sacred sweep of its understanding of history?

What magazines do you subscribe to? What books do you purchase? What libraries do you use? What are your study habits?

When was the last time you wrote a sermon, word for word, giving careful attention to its structure, its style and economy of verbage, then immersed yourself in it (as Maclaren did) so that its delivery seemed natural and spontaneous and its impact upon its hearers was dramatic and compelling?

You won't do things as Maclaren did, nor should you. But, what equivalent disciplines have you cultivated that you might faithfully relate biblical truth to the people committed to your care and help set the stage for dramatic change? John Wesley and Alexander Maclaren, radically different in almost every respect, were *biblical* preachers. Although we live in the waning years of the twentieth century we are called to be the same. Fifteen years ago an obscure young preacher wrote, "When the worshipping community is prepared for God's righteous action in their midst by the prophetic word on the preacher's tongue, they can be strong in the faith and confident of victory. The Bible is the book of the church when the preacher lets it preach to the church."

Faithful biblical preaching can be explosive. It is therefore wise to anticipate the consequences of such preaching. Those who are calling us "back to the Bible" may not understand the implications of their plea. When the Bible is believed, is accepted as authority, the results are transforming. Jim Wallis, editor of *Sojourners,* is one of the "young evangelicals" who is breathing new life into the dry bones of yesteryear. In his *Agenda for Biblical People* he writes:

> The central biblical tension between "this age" and the "age to come" is the political key, the decisive factor of radical social change in history. Revolution is founded upon the premise that something is basically wrong with the world and springs from a vision of change and hope that has been seen beyond the present circumstances and conditions of history. Confident faith in the power of a future reality is hardly a social opiate that encourages passive acceptance of the status quo, but rather is the very engine and dynamo of revolutionary expectation and action.*

"The "real world" referred to in chapter one, the world that challenges academicians and social critics, must be seen in biblical perspective. To "preach the Bible" is to loose its liberating power in those political, economic, cultural, and personal domains where people function.

However, truth is more than biblical. Old Bishop Quayle used to take a market basket into downtown Chicago every Monday morning, fill it with secondhand books from the bookstores, and charter his study course for the week. A critical Scottish visitor, as he looked at the habits of our clergy, once said, "You Americans spend more on gas than the books you read." Right now, in the light of

---

*Jim Wallis, *Agenda for Biblical People,* (New York: Harper and Row, 1976), p. 132.

energy crises and soaring costs, that may be necessary.
But the lesson is clear. The most effective and influential
clergy of this or any other day are those who take the time
and invest the necessary energy to expand the borders of
their minds.

Nor do you have to be a Ph.D. to do this. You don't
need the impressive scholarly credentials of a Maclaren or
a Wesley. One of the greatest preachers of this century
was J. Wallace Hamilton. When I began as a student
preacher in Florida thirty years ago, Dr. Hamilton was in
his prime, less than forty miles from my "appointment."
What a legend to brush elbows with. "Ham," as he was
affectionately called, never attended a university or a
theological school. Norman Vincent Peale once said Hamilton was the best argument he had ever met for preachers *not* going to seminary. Charles Clayton Morrison, in
an article contending that Hamilton had "overtaken" the
likes of Buttrick, Bosley, Elson, McCracken, and Sock-
man, explained his remarkable development:

> [Hamilton's] entire formal education above his
> Canadian high school consisted of two and a
> half years at Moody Bible Institute . . . from
> which he graduated (in 1924). . . . Yet (his)
> mind has traversed the identical route which
> Christian thought has taken in the past half-
> century. . . . In the 1920s he came under the
> influence of the social gospel to which he gave
> intense allegiance. . . . Such books as those of
> Jeans and Eddington saved him from the pitfall
> of scientific absolutism and thrust him into the
> study of philosophy that was then emerging
> from its bondage to the scientific method. Thus
> he found himself drawn into the orbit of philo-
> sophical theology represented by Tillich and
> Niebuhr, and especially by Martin Buber. . . .
> Dr. Hamilton's theological pilgrimage describes
> in a personal experience of thirty mature years

the route which Christian thought has taken in
the past half-century.*

As is evident, Wallace Hamilton was a disciplined student. He guarded his time in his study like a watchdog
protecting crown jewels. Serving a drive-in church in
Florida, he preached to thousands of people every Sunday.
And what a sermonic diet he offered them. Read his *Ride
the Wild Horses*, his *Thunder of Bare Feet*, his *Serendip-
ity* and *Still the Trumpet Sounds*. The social gospel is
there; the personal gospel is there. The informed mind is
there as is the warmth of life-centeredness. As Frank
Mead once wrote:

> Hamilton has no sermon barrel. It is preaching
> with no inferiority complex, no apology. It is
> vibrant and alive. . . . It listens to psychol-
> ogy. . . . It is versed in science. . . . It is replete
> with illustrations from the best of literature. . . .
> There is common sense and good humor and a
> language as plain and understandable as the
> language of the New Testament.

You may be self-conscious about your lack of formal
training or your lack of graduate credentials. Take heart!
One of the most effective pulpit voices of our time had no
formal training beyond a few courses taken in a funda-
mentalist school. Take heart—*but not too much,* unless
you are willing to pay the price he paid. He grew. He
grew beyond those early years and the primitive ideas of
his early training. He grew because he immersed himself
in the traditions of the past and the emergence of new insights and movements. He seemed to understand that
learning truth is a never-ending process.

There is a sense in which the minister, more than any

---

*The Christian Century, August 5, 1959, p. 904.

other professional in contemporary society, is privileged to be a Renaissance person; that is, a person whose interests run the gamut of experience and reality. As Michelangelo and Leonardo da Vinci of old, the preacher's mind can grapple with the dominant themes of existence: with creation and "the fall," justice and judgment, culture and ethics, space conquest and geo-politics. The urban minister can study the dynamics of urban life, drugs and crime, racism, community organization and metropolitan government, housing and patterns of employment. The rural minister can learn about family farms, corporate structures, and agri-business, food production and distribution, hunger and fertilizers, and the "green revolution." Dependent upon our needs and commitments we can apply ourselves to politics on Capitol Hill and in the State House, the plight of the Native American, the rights of women, the charismatic movement and pentecostalism, human sexuality, ecumenism and the rebirth of Roman Catholicism, technology and modern communications systems, the delicate balance of a fragile ecosystem, the "power of the Pentagon" and the apocalyptic possibilities of nuclear warfare, liberation movements and the grim prospects of endangered species (including people like us). Do you fully realize what a range of possibilities present-day ministry holds for those who are called to share its treasures? Phillips Brooks, in his Beecher lectures, said:

> The Christian ministry is the largest field for growth of a human soul that this world offers. In it [those who are] faithful must go on learning more and more forever.

He also said:

There is no career that can compare with it for a moment in the rich and satisfying relationships into which it brings a man with his fellow man, in the deep and interesting insights which it gives him into human nature, and in the choice of the best culture for his own nurture. Its delight never grows old, its interest never wanes, its stimulus is never exhausted.

Of course, this opens up new vistas for learning truth. Not only are we committed to the disciplines of book learning and Bible study; there is the ever fertile and indispensable field of "rich and satisfying (human) relationships."

We learn by observing life, by relating to people, by participating in significant events. Eyes, ears, and instruments of retention become basic tools of our trade.

In Henry Miller's *Plexus* the author is transformed into an enormous eye. He says, "The moment one gives close attention to anything, even a blade of grass, it becomes a mysterious, awesome, indescribably magnified world in itself." In his youth, while riding on trolley cars and subways, Miller would read "faces . . . gestures . . . gaits . . . architecture, streets, passions, crimes. Everything . . . was noted, analyzed, compared, and described—for future use." That is another way truth is learned.

Two of the most widely read and influential American novelists of the twentieth century have been John Steinbeck and Ernest Hemingway. Steinbeck, although he went to Stanford off and on for five years, never took a degree. He didn't particularly want one; he was too busy living. While a student he was also a road worker, rancher, a hod carrier, dockhand, and cotton picker. He even helped build Madison Square Garden on an early eastern jaunt. He grew up in, became part of, and never really left

Salinas Valley with its migrant workers and Monterey paisanos. He prepared himself for *The Grapes of Wrath* by following migrants from Oklahoma to California, by living with them and coming to identify with their struggles and heartaches. He learned the truths he explored in his masterful stories by roaming over and becoming one with a rough and demanding terrain.

The same can be said of Hemingway. In a moving tribute Archibald MacLeish wrote:

> Hemingway was not a watcher; he was an actor in his life. *He took part.* He could never go to war—and he went to every war available to him—without engaging in it. He went to the First World War as an ambulance driver and got his knee smashed by a shell in a front line trench where no one had sent him. He went to Spain to write a scenario for a movie and learned how you washed the powder burns off your hands without water. He went to the last World War as a correspondent—and worried the high command by turning up with tools other than typewriters—mementoes he called them. And between wars there were lions and elephants. And between lions and elephants there were marlin. Also bears. . . .

Ernest Hemingway lived what he wrote about, including his bizarre fascination with violence and with death. So the question follows: does the minister enter into those relationships and participate in those events that give substance, meaning, and authority to words uttered and causes pled for? My experience has been relatively limited, but I can detail for you where some of the most valuable and dramatic education of my life has taken place.

I learned about "revivalism" not by reading sociology

textbooks or the sermons of Dwight L. Moody and Billy Graham, or by enjoying Sinclair Lewis' *Elmer Gantry*, but by holding "meetings." As a young preacher I held revivals across the Southland. I still conduct preaching missions each year attempting to fulfill that part of my calling while staying in close touch with the people who are the church.

I learned about race relations and the "black revolution," not by reading Eric Lincoln or Malcolm X, Eldridge Cleaver, or James Cone (although I did that), but by serving a church in a black neighborhood, visiting in black homes, marching with blacks during civil rights days and getting to know black prisoners in the penitentiaries of Indiana. I have read Vine Deloria, Jr., but I also went to the Pine Ridge during the siege of Wounded Knee in 1973, and have stood by the sides of Native Americans as they sought to articulate their grievances and gain just redress for the tragic sins of the past.

The war in Vietnam? The books were there and I read them. But there was a trip to Saigon in 1969—there were the Vietnamese prisons visited, the sounds and stench of war in the air, and the children's hospital with its moans and cries of agony. There were trips to Paris during the "peace talks." There were the protest marches and prayer vigils and fasts. And there was a visit to Hanoi and points south in the spring of 1976. That was all a part of learning truth.

I would guess I've read as much about politics as I have theology over the past ten years. But the education hasn't been limited to books written by Schlesinger, Becker, and Theodore White. There was poll watching on Indiana Avenue in the heart of an Indianapolis ghetto, and reform politics in a city of 700,000, and the primaries of '68, and the presidential campaign of '72, and a rather lively 1974 senatorial campaign in South Dakota. There have been speech writing and brainstorming, strategy planning and arm-bending; there have been warm friendships and unbelievable heartaches and joyous moments of victory shared. All of this has been a part of learning truth.

I remember what an emotional experience it used to be to go into the Broadway pulpit I served for a decade in Indianapolis. My eyes would scan the congregation. There was the young widow trying valiantly to be mother, father, breadwinner, and friend. There was the taxi driver who had had his troubles with the law and his own undisciplined habits. There was the interracial couple with the small children who didn't seem to belong anywhere, and who wanted so desperately to belong. The mayor was there as were the county chairpersons of both political parties. There were the women I had baptized, women released from the state prison for women. There were the families—so very many families—struggling to make a go of it against the worst of odds. And the homosexuals, the public servants, the lonely saints, and the hardened sinners; the youngsters stumbling through adolescence and the senior citizens afraid of uncertain tomorrows. Those were days in which I was reading Bultmann and Barth, the young Bob Raines and Ted Webber, the brothers Niebuhr and Bishop Pike. But the truth I was learning, the *fundamental* truth I was learning, was centered in the drama of those human lives I was privileged to interact with day after hectically busy day.

And when I mounted the steps going up into that Broadway pulpit, do you know what I saw? A sign, visible only to me, that said, "Let them see God!" That is the mission of ministry now as always. *Let the people see God!* Through the flawed imperfections of our selfhood and our finitude and relative grasp of eternal truth the people are entitled to gain authentic glimpses of the One who gives meaning to their lives.

James Black used to say, "In the ministry of all places God has no use for a lazy person." Be what you are called to be. Meet the demands. Pay the price. Offer yourself as a living sacrifice. Set about to learn truth, in every responsible way possible, that others might come to know fullness of life because of the integrity and vitality of your openness, growth and faithful servanthood.

Chapter Three

Chapter Three

Doing Truth

Truth + personality + the ability to communicate = preaching: that is the formula Phillips Brooks gave us. In the last chapter we discussed the vagaries of truth. We have yet to explore the power and mystique of verbal communication. But before that we must deal with the key to the whole process—the *person* through whom the words of truth must be transmitted. The person. Robert McCracken, Harry Emerson Fosdick's successor at Riverside Church in New York, once said, "Essential as it is that [the preacher] should prepare his sermon it is even more essential that he should prepare himself." The person. It was said of the Roman philosopher, Seneca, "His thoughts [were] excellent if only he had the right to utter them." The person. The Christian faith is incarnational. The Word became flesh. Authentic proclamation cannot be disembodied. We who bear the good tidings are called to reflect, in our own personhood, the message we presume to proclaim.

Francis Bacon possessed one of the most impressive intellects England has produced. During the early days of Shakespearan scholarship it was assumed by many that a man named Shakespeare never lived. Only Francis Bacon, they reasoned, knew enough to write the works attributed to the Bard of Avon. Bacon redirected the course of philosophy and scientific theory. He wrote voluminously about history, literature, and law. Yet, as our Pilgrim foreparents were trying to survive their first grim winter in the New World, Francis Bacon was impeached as Lord Chancellor of the British Crown for judicial corruption. The poet, Pope, called him "the wisest, wittiest, meanest of mankind." He was a brilliant man, but the quality of his life did not reflect the genius of his mind.

That, of course, is what Watergate was all about. The administration of President Richard M. Nixon was projected as one of unswerving fidelity and honor. The White House worship services were symbols of its noble purpose. There was an ecumenical corps of "chaplains" surrounding the White House guard: Billy Graham and Norman Vincent Peale, representing the uncritical status quo of the Protestant center; the Jesuit priest on the White House payroll, Father John McLaughlin, who one day told a reporter, "President Nixon is a man of simple, honest piety" (that same day it was revealed that the President had been involved in the cover-up from the beginning); and the strange little rabbi, Baruch Korff, who seemed to believe more "impossible things" than anyone since the adventures of Alice in Wonderland. Who can forget John Ehrlichman testifying before the Senate Watergate Committee, self-righteously regaling our nation's lawmakers for imbibing in intoxicants? Who can forget John Mitchell, who had been the chief law enforcement officer of the land, unctuously saying no fate could have been worse, in the fall of 1972, than a victory for Senator McGovern at the polls? These two men, and a host of cronies and underlings, conspired to commit criminal deeds against the people of the United States because they had convinced themselves of the righteousness of their power. By and large they were persons of high private morality, but they had no sense of public morality; of ethical responsibility. They filled the air with self-serving preachments all the while approving and engaging in criminal activities, invading the privacy and violating the rights of American citizens and undermining the Constitution of the United States.

Some time ago an article appeared in the *Washingtonian* about "God and Man in Washington" with the subtitle: "How Religion is Used and Abused in the Eternal City of Politics." The author, a cynical sort, made short shrift of much of the religiosity in our nation's capitol. He was amused by the naïvete of the followers of the Reverend Sun Myung Moon, the Korean evangelist; disgusted by the pompous rhetoric of the clergy chaplains of the House and Senate; amazed by the sanctified audacity and downright crookedness of the Watergate crew. But, he couldn't cope with Senator Harold Hughes of Iowa. Hughes almost got to him. The senator, about to leave the Senate for a fulltime religious work, talked to the reporter about Christ, prayed with him; said, "God has touched you here this morning and you have a choice. You will leave this room having decided one way or another." And the reporter wrote, "I could feel God. I could feel God. I could feel God within Hughes. I could feel God in the room. . . ."

According to his friends on Capitol Hill, Harold Hughes

left his Senate seat for two reasons. First, he had been a very effective governor of his state. He was accustomed to power. He could lift his telephone in Des Moines, make a few well-placed calls and initiate change —he could get things done. He came to Washington in a flurry and exercised remarkable influence as a freshman senator, but he was frustrated by his relative impotence. A lawmaker is not a chief executive. By temperament Hughes was not a patient man and found it virtually impossible to fit his urgent drives and restless ideals into the job description of a United States senator. But second, and this his friends respect, Christ had become more and more real to him. Christ was calling him to a new task. His very personhood was involved. No one questioned his sincerity. Somehow his words and life had to come together in closer harmony. The Harold Hughes phenomena has much to say to those of us who are called to "communicate truth."

In all of this—a remembrance of the "fatal flaw" in Francis Bacon, a theological awareness of the implications of Watergate and a brief glimpse at the career of Harold Hughes, from alcoholic truck driver to governor's mansion, to Capitol Hill, to role as full-time Christian worker, we are reminded of the basic ingredients of the gospel. However we choose to define "original sin" the fact remains: we are not what we ought to be, not one of us, and our human failure consists of more than misused freedom and deliberate rebellion. We are, by nature, self-seeking and self-serving. Even our self-righteousness (no, *especially* our self-righteousness) is a measure of the nature and extent of our "fall." But, *Christ can save!* This we preach. This is the very core of our tradition. Yet, as clergy we sometimes fail to embrace this fundamental promise in our own lives. Communicating truth to others we do not claim its liberating power for ourselves and so deny ourselves those resources of grace and integrity without which personal growth is unlikely.

In our ministries we are challenged to cultivate (that means: to "grow," "tend," "nurture," "foster," "form," "refine") *our own personhood.* In a world gone mad we are called upon to reflect stability and sanity. In the words of the Apostle: "The whole created universe groans in all its parts . . . while we wait for God to make us . . . [wholly] free. For we have been saved" (Rom. 8:22–24 NEB). "The love of Christ leaves us no choice. . . . When anyone is united to Christ there is a new world" (2 Cor. 5:14, 17 NEB). He or she is a "new being."

It does not require a special form of knowledge to see the radical difference between the 1960s and the 1970s. In the sixties we were caught up in the civil rights movement and the peace movement, in the new politics and the "greening of America." We were activists entertaining bold decisions, running risks, defying entrenched power, making our lonely stands. That is not the mood of the seventies. Suddenly, we have become "spiritual." The Jesus movement and the charismatic movement spread as a flame across the land. Eastern mysticism with its gurus and holy men, its yoga and trancendental meditation, its radical turn inward has piqued our curiosity and stimulated our soul-hunger.

If only we could bring the best of the sixties and seventies together. We need the impatient idealism, prophetic judgment and commitment to genuine, systemic change of the sixties—but our activism back then had too few roots. Much of it had no grounding in the bedrock of a sustaining, transforming faith. We need the spiritual sensitivity of the seventies—if we can just overcome its selfish instincts and self-deifying tendencies, and claim the newness of life it offers. As Emilio Castro has said, "How do we rediscover the eternal Christian truth that the gospel is not for our enjoyment but for others." The gospel is for others, but it is only a verbal showpiece unless it is first appropriated *in our own persons.*

Lest we react against that which is so personal and subjective in the current mood, let's confess our needs. Several years ago there was a Broadway play called *Merrily We Roll Along.* Its opening scene described the life and times of Richard Miles, a successful playwright. Mr. Miles was a success as the world defines success, but his ideals had deteriorated and his behavior, his personal life-style, had become shameful and degrading. The play depicted the life of Richard Miles in reverse. Each succeeding scene and act showed Miles younger and finer. The action traveled back over the road into the past until, at last, the characters were sharing Miles' college commencement. Richard Miles was the class valedictorian. As the final curtain went down Miles was saying, "Lastly, this I have learned: I have learned to value ideals above all else. Let them be our heritage, our guiding force." Do we see ourselves in such reflection? Is our motivation today, our commitment today, our "purity of heart" today what once it was?

What if we "succeed" as ministers, moving "up the ladder," gaining impressive reputations, exercising ever wider influence—what if we thrill people from our pulpits, win their approval and adulation, and guide our congregations and co-workers into constructive ministries in the world—and with the passage of time become less and less "Christian"? Or—what if we simply muddle along, moving from one community to another, one assignment to another, with predictable concerns and complaints, never really feeling fulfilled, knowing our share of disappointment and resentment yet never quite acknowledging their presence because such emotions seem unworthy of us? Through it all, whether our churches are large or small, whether our tasks are challenging or seem mundane and commonplace, who and where are we in the process of becoming persons? Do we appear to be, in motive and manner, new creatures in Christ? Do we reflect his spirit? Do we radiate and share his unselfish love? Is the core of our personhood authentic and stable? Or, in reality, does there seem to be little difference between the quality of life we boast and that of the sinful worldling who lives next door?

Richard Miles, the playwright, changed with the passage of time. But then, we all do, one way or another. As Cardinal Newman said, life is change; "life is growth." We are in the process of becoming what we one day will be. That is the wondrous dynamic of human nature. The only clue to our Lord's adolescence and young adulthood is captured in the brief word: "He *grew* in wisdom and stature and favor with God and man." He grew. He developed. In relationship to God and others he cultivated his personhood.

As communicators many of us are like the young Emil Brunner. He said that before he encountered Crisis Theology he felt like a sandwich board man parading the streets with an advertisement for the best of food draped over his shoulders—and all the while he, the bearer of the word, was hungry.

How do we become what we are called to be? I know of no way to improve upon the classic gospel formula.

We *repent;* that is, while celebrating and affirming the gift of life we acknowledge the frailty and limitations of our humanity, the various hues and shades of our attitudes and motives, and the "exceeding sinfulness" of our sins.

We acknowledge the painful reality of our spiritual and intellectual arrogance, of our phony postures and frail efforts. We pinpoint and agonize over those specific moods and happenings that violate trust relationships and blaspheme sacred responsibilities. We repent.

We *believe;* that is, we embrace with heart, soul, mind and strength, with the energies of our lives, the reality of the love of God as revealed in Jesus Christ. We, the clergy, accept him as the Lord of our lives and the Savior and Fulfillment of our promise and potential. We take the "leap of faith," abandoning the security of the culturally approved; the cheaply popular; the personally safe. We believe.

And—we *grow in grace.* This does not happen automatically. It was said of the artist, Augustus John, that "slowly something vital drained out of his work—confidence, perhaps, or energy, or the sure technique—until, at the end, he had become a sad self-imitator, miserably aware of what he had failed to reach." That, in a sense, is what happened to Richard Miles—and it happens to many of us. Personhood must be *cultivated.* The fragile garden of the spirit must be tended if the fruits of the spirit—love, joy, peace, patience, kindness, goodness, fidelity, gentleness, and self-control—are to become integral parts of who we really are. This cultivation requires honesty and humility, reflection, meditation and dispassionate inwardness. It is the gift of grace, the fruit of that God-conscious, other-centered way of life some call prayer. Growth in grace—"holiness of heart and life" (as Wesley defined it)—the capacity to be a mature and fully-functioning person result from our commitment to Christ and our life with him.

Before we can communicate the truth, authentically, we must come to an awareness of where we are moving, of what we are becoming, and to some degree, of who we really are. *In a moment of time when identity crises are the vogue it is essential that we determine as best we can our individual identities and then cling to that knowledge come what may.*

Granted, some of us have more than our share of anxieties and neuroses. In the face of personal stress, family tension and professional groping we can be frightfully insecure. This is exactly why we need to think through the nature of our personhood in relationship to God and his creation and then refuse to sell out to lesser claims and definitions.

I have mentioned the "spirituality" of the seventies. Much of it is simply navel gazing, the transference of self-centeredness to the realm of the spirit. Bypassing the "imputed righteousness" and disciplines of holy living our tradition instructs us in, we are caught up in a fascinating variety of self-salvation schemes: transactional analysis, transcendental meditation, ESP, psychokinesis, the new morality, the new secularity, some form of political or economic salvation. Somehow, in the context of Gethsemane, the prayer, "I'm OK—You're OK" doesn't quite ring true.

Peter Marin, writing in *Harper's,* discussed "The New Narcissism." He argued that many approaches to psychotherapy in the recent past have been "silly" and "boring." Now, however, some are becoming downright self-destructive. With legitimate emphases upon personal identity and the fulfillment of human potential they tend to veer off in directions that are morally irresponsible and unashamedly self-centered. A vital religious faith has been replaced by a fuzzy-headed determination to do "one's own thing"—whatever that may mean or be. Marin wrote that ". . . selfishness and moral blindness now assert themselves . . . as enlightenment and psychic health." It is never healthy to bow down before the altar on which the idol of the self is perched. The indignant activism of the sixties did not save the world. The self-adulation and rampant emotionalism of the seventies won't save it either. The reality of God, his infinite love, his sovereign grace, the gift and witness of his Spirit—these are the realities that give both word and life meaning. How can we grow in grace if we don't believe in it? rely upon it? gratefully and humbly accept it?

One of Phillips Brooks' lectures on preaching dealt with "the preacher himself." Brooks was a creature of his time and therefore did not deal with some of the critical issues that besiege us, but he knew his clergy. He suggested, at a very practical level, two ever-present temptations in the minister's world: "self-conceit" and "self-indulgence."

Self-conceit: I have known some conceited ministers, not all that many, but some. They have been over-impressed by their native abilities, their arts and skills, their public relations prowess and capacity to "get things done." Joseph Parker, the famous orator of City Temple, London, was once asked by a fledgling preacher if he would come to the young man's suburban chapel and help dedicate it. Parker curtly replied, "Can an eagle sit on a sparrow's nest?" I have not known too many "eagles" in the ministry; some perhaps, but not many. (But then I have also known "hawks," "chickens," and even a sprinkling of "vultures.") Often, our apparent conceit is but a cover-up for feelings of inadequacy. It is overcompensation. Even so, Jesus saved his sharpest barbs for the self-impressed Pharisees. He said, "Blessed are the poor in spirit"—"the humble-minded"—"the teachable." Genuine servanthood and extravagant conceit are mutually exclusive phrases.

And then there is **self-indulgence.** The laziness we talked about earlier is a form of self-indulgence. A minister who is immobilized by the whining demands of those about him, the nagging pressures of a self-assertive parishioner or his own spiritual ambivalence cannot be effective. But, self-indulgence is more than weakness and uncertainty. It may result from an erroneous self-concept or from the groveling posture of a sycophant. Brooks said, "It (is) not good that the minister should be worshipped and made an oracle. It is still worse that he should be flattered and made a pet." He went on to say, "Resent indulgences which are not given to persons of other professions. . . . Never appeal for sympathy. . . . Count your manliness [and womanliness] the soul of your ministry and resist all attacks upon it however sweetly they may come." Determine who you are and cling to that self-knowledge. Don't let anyone make of you a neuter, a member of some mythical third sex, a godly oddball who is neither fish nor fowl. For God's sake, embrace the gift of life; be *yourself!*

Students of church history tend to dehumanize the giants of the past. They gloss over Calvin's cruelty and the hell of Wesley's home life. They disregard Martin Luther's anti-Semitism and his infatuation with the princes of his day. They also lose sight of the lusty warmth of the man. One biographer, R. W. Dale, said of Luther:

> He was a man and he didn't try to be anything else. . . . He had flesh and blood; he could not help it. He did not desire to help it. He ate heartily and enjoyed his friends. He married a wife and loved her. . . . He liked music and songs as well as preaching and sermons.

He loved people and nature and his country. His body and soul were not divided. He was who he was, without apology.

David Riesman, who appeared on the scene long after Martin Luther and Phillips Brooks, provided fresh insights into our selfhood. In his influential book, *The Lonely Crowd*, he talked about people who are "outer-directed." The outer-directed person is one who "lives as though he were directed by a radar set fastened to his head perpetually telling him what other people expect of him." Think of the implications with reference to ministry.

People expect you to sound religious. Sound religious.

People expect you to be sweet and sentimental. Appear to be sweet and sentimental.

Critics say you must be profane and worldly. All right, be profane and worldly. How many young clergy, and some of their older counterparts, feel they have to swear and drink more, "swing" more, be more "worldly" than those around them to prove their down-to-earth humanity? They are just as outer-directed as the sober, pious, pompous colleagues they are reacting against. Be who you are. To employ Riesman's terminology, be inner-directed; live as though you were given stability and direction by an inner gyroscope. Let that inner world of yours determine your stance and your reactions.

This slender volume is designed to probe the ways and means of communication, but *proclamation cannot, dare not, be divorced from incarnation.* God was in Christ. The Word was made flesh. The creed is meaningless apart from the deed. Verbalization becomes blaspheme when removed from the honest reality of one's inner world.

Some time ago I was asked to keynote the annual meeting of a major denomination's council on evangelism. I was assigned the topic, "His Word through Preaching" and was told to "talk about preaching . . . demonstrate preaching . . . emphasize preaching." I reneged—that is, I didn't stick to the assigned topic. I said there is no way to separate the Word from the flesh. We have no right to disembody proclamation. As a recent definition of evangelism put it, "The good news flows freely from the words and life-styles of faith *embodied in persons. . . .* People are not called to believe something so much as to be a part of something."

What are we called to be a part of? The very life of Christ. He is our authority, our model, the basis and inspiration of our radical discipleship.

Compare the ways of our Lord with the moods and aspirations that drive most of us.

He was born, not in a royal nursery, but in a stable, a cave, surrounded by the stench and sounds of dumb animals.

He was a peasant, not a scribe nor a Pharisee, not a rabbi nor a banker, not a prince nor a captain of industry, but a lowly peasant tradesman.

His moment of greatest earthly triumph came as he entered the Holy City on the back of an ass. (How the philosopher, Nietzsche, loved to ridicule that symbolism!) Jesus was no five-star general; no marauding conqueror. Palm Sunday did not exalt the "power of the Pentagon"— only the truth present in a humble carpenter on a borrowed beast of burden.

And when it came time to die he died on a cross between two common criminals, executed on a garbage dump outside the city walls. The militant grandeur of "The Hallelujah Chorus" would come later—much, much later.

Think of the implications of all this if an incarnational faith is taken seriously. Don't misunderstand me. I am not denigrating the place of the pulpit or the power of the spoken word. As we have already suggested, we need to be more disciplined and impassioned, not less, as we consider communicating the truth of the living Word. But phrases like "pulpit prince" and "the royalty of the pulpit" are contradictions in terms. We are called to bear witness to the truth; to testify on behalf of one who was lowly and nonviolent, caring and humble, one who became *nothing* for the sake of all of us. He was a man for others, a responsible, sensitive, suffering servant.

You see, the preaching of the Word becomes authentic only as it takes on the flesh of our full humanity. Pulpit oratory is the cheapest possible substitute for faithful discipleship. A sermon may *convey* the Word, but—with all of his or her acknowledged failings—the preacher is called upon to *be* the Word; to *do* and *live* the truth.

In my early ministry I worshiped at the shrine of an earthbound trinity: Robertson of Brighton, Phillips Brooks and Harry Emerson Fosdick. They, more than any others, shaped my tastes and loyalties. I studied their sermons diligently and sought to learn from them. One day I read of a sermon called by one observer the most eloquent sermon Phillips Brooks ever preached. It had nothing to do with the spoken word or with the pulpit of Trinity Parish in Boston. He simply walked through Harvard Square. And the students, looking at him, saw and heard the essential Word. His personhood had become his sermon—and they responded. That is how it ought to be with us. We must *do* the truth, *live* the truth, even as we seek to verbalize the message. As Robert Mc-Cracken said, "Essential as it is that [the preacher] should prepare the sermon, it is even more important that the self should be prepared."

Chapter Four

Chapter Four

Preaching Truth

It's not easy to be a preacher today, at least the kind of preacher this day needs—one whose voice is certain, whose faith is vibrant, whose mind is informed and whose hope is real and constant. Ironically, the old iconoclast George Bernard Shaw saw himself as something of a preacher, but he was a preacher who had been buffeted about by the cruel realities of a violent world. In "Too Good to Be True," he said:

> I am by nature and destiny a preacher. . . . But I have no Bible, no creed; the war has shot both out of my hands. The war has been a fiery forcing house in which we've grown with a rush like flowers in a late spring following a terrible winter. And with what result? This: that we have outgrown our religion, outgrown our political system, outgrown our strength of mind and character. The fatal word NOT has been in-

scribed into all our creeds. . . . But, what next? Is NO enough? Is NO enough? For a boy, yes; for a man, never. . . . I must have affirmations to preach. . . . The preacher must preach the way of life—Oh, if I could only find it!

To find the way of life, to find it and communicate it—that is our calling.

Again let me remind you: Phillips Brooks said, "Preaching is the bringing of truth through personality." He added, "Neither of these can it spare and still be preaching." How overwhelming the challenge; how inadequate we seem when trying to accept it. Truth? That, in part at least, has cosmic connotations. It has dimensions that are ever beyond us. Personality? That is a sacred gift defying natural explanations and definitions. How can the two be brought together that the Word might be proclaimed? With realism and with humility. Listen to this description of the preacher:

> He stands between the ever
> And the now—
> A slender, tender,
> Fragile coupling.
>
> Through him pass the yearnings
> Of the bruised and battered
> Sons of earth—
> The fervid hopes and prayers
> Of cosmic neophytes
> Perplexed and lost and lonely,
> Clamoring for comfort
> And hungering for courage
> In communion with the soul of souls.
>
> Through him comes, returning,
> That strange mysterious flood
> Of power—
> The stream of hope and healing,
> The word of everlasting wisdom,
> The hand outstretched. . . .

And there is none but Christ
With whom to share his anguish
As he finds himself
Too slender
Too tender
Too fragile.

In realism and humility the preacher must realize just how fragile, how tender, is the personal instrumentality God would use. We understand, and on occasion have echoed the plaintive cry of the Irish playwright: "If only I could find . . . the way of life." We can understand the plaintive cry, but we dare not stop there. Honest humility is one thing; false humility, quite another. "We are the leaders of people," said Brooks. "Woe to our preaching if in any feeble, false humility we abdicate that place."

The message we proclaim is a "given" message. It is drawn from the Bible and books, from journals and conversations and people. It is a life-centered message. But it is also gospel proclamation. Unlike George Bernard Shaw, we have not permitted chaos and disaster to take our message from us.

We proclaim the *fact* of God, the *fact* of Christ, the *fact* that God in Christ can meet his own, wherever they are, cleanse and refashion them, and redirect the world of which they are a part.

There is no need to catalog the crises of our time: the arms race with its balance-of-terror and possibility of nuclear holocaust, worldwide hunger and the threat of mass starvation, economic injustice and wars of liberation, political tyranny and oppression, an age-old lust for power and the collapse of traditional moral values. But, ours is not a purposeless, rudderless, drifting, foredoomed universe. It belongs to God. *God is!* He is alive and with us. His name and nature are love, and he is ever available to us. He has revealed himself in myriad ways, but most especially—from our vantage point—in the person and work of Christ. God was in Christ. The Word was made flesh and dwelt among us. The gospel insists that God is not a distant, ethereal concept—an oblong blur in a far-away sky. He is one with us in the stuff of our own existence, striving with us, suffering and overcoming with us. Christ the Savior, Christ the Lord, has brought God, the Creator and Sustainer of all life, into the immediate orbit of our personal, historic experience.

Proclamation is the declaration of the Good News that life can be radically different—we can become new creatures—the created order can be refashioned into a new heaven and a new earth. God's will, his reign of justice and love can be done here and now, in measured and relative ways, even as it is known in the eternal beyond.

The preacher has a Word to preach, a saving truth that can be transmitted through personality.

But, there is more to preaching than the "kerygma." There is more to the mailing of a letter than the letter itself. There is the stationery, the envelope and the stamp. There is the Postal Service. There is the sender and receiver.

We have talked about the preacher, the sender. But what of *the receiver, the people, the waiting congregation*? Preaching is not preaching apart from that waiting congregation.

A biographer once said of Phillips Brooks, "He loved places and things, he loved nature, but above all he loved humanity. It was this gift that made his heart leap up when he beheld the waiting congregation. No one can forget the look he gave when he ascended the pulpit, as if to draw in the inspiration for the effect that was to follow before he bent himself with the fervor and tumult of his powerful soul to the communication of his message."

I have already confessed that Frederick W. Robertson, Phillips Brooks and Harry Emerson Fosdick comprised a sort of earthbound trinity for me during the early years of my ministry. Fosdick reacted to people much as did Brooks. Fosdick once wrote, "Let the preacher begin with the people in front of him, with what goes on inside of them." He also said, "Preaching is wrestling with individuals over questions of life and death, and until that idea of it commands a preacher's mind and method, eloquence will avail him little and theology not at all."

I am in the ministry today primarily because of a man named P. M. Boyd. He brought me back into the church after early and bitter rebellion. Born in North Georgia he was as "southern" as sow-belly and fat-back. He was a brilliant organizer; an unbelievable money-raiser; a conference politician without peer. (I knew none of these things about him when he entered my life.) His preaching was remarkably like that of Clovis Chappel, complete with the spontaneous humor and homey illustrations. But, above all else, P. M. Boyd loved people. He began as my minister. Then, when I was a student preacher, he was my district superintendent. When I graduated from seminary I returned to Florida to be his associate pastor in Jacksonville. For three years I saw him work with people, suffer and bleed with people, *love* people. He was the greatest, most sensitive shepherd of souls I have ever known. He once told me what to say at his funeral. He said, "Tell them I love God, The Methodist Church and people—especially children." He died, at the age of eighty-six, in October, 1975. Hundreds of people, from every walk of life, filled the church in Jacksonville to

overflowing. They *celebrated* his meaning and ministry.
And, as I shared with them what he had told me to say
they nodded in affirmation. Dr. Boyd was one of the most
effective ministers I have ever known. He had little formal
training, but how he did love people. And they knew it.
His preaching was a conversation with beloved friends.
He laughed, fished, hunted, and wept with them through
the days of the week; he shared their decisions, bore their
burdens and suffered their humanity through the days of
the week—and on Sunday, knowing and loving them as
he did, he proclaimed the Word in ways that met them
exactly where they were and drew them into the very
presence of God. That's preaching! We can talk about
homiletics, about cultivating the arts and skills of preaching, but divorced from gut-level pastoral instincts they
are nothing.

> I may speak with the tongues of men or of
> angels. . . . I may have the gift of prophecy and
> know every hidden truth; I may have faith
> strong enough to move mountains; but if I have
> no love, I am nothing (1 Cor. 13:1–3, NEB).

Those people out there, people for whom Christ died, are
the reasons for our being. They are the ones to whom we
are called and for whom we minister.

The receiver, the waiting congregation, is a vital
ingredient in the communication of the gospel. So is the
sender (as I suggested in chapter three), the one who
writes the letter, who prepares the message, who trans-
mits the Word. *But, how does one compose that message?
How does one prepare the sermon?*

Not by simply observing life as it passes by, although
a poetic, historic awareness of life processes is important.

Don't forget Henry Miller's "eye" in *Plexus* scanning the horizon, drinking in all that is observable, attempting to digest and interpret that which others tend to ignore or see with only a passing glance.

Nor is a sermon prepared in the study alone. But for the sake of everything you have committed your life to in ministry, don't neglect your study. No two of you will work out the mechanics of sermon preparation in exactly the same way. Alexander Maclaren argued that sixty hours a week should be devoted to sermon preparation. As recent a pulpit master as Harold Bosley pled for an investment of from thirty to forty hours a week in a sermon. J. Wallace Hamilton locked himself away from administrative and pastoral duties hours on end, day after day, and slaved over the details of each sermon designed to be delivered from his Pasadena Community pulpit. Yet, much as I admire the discipline and craftsmanship of these preachers extraordinary, let me suggest a practical, workable alternative, one that will allow for intensive pastoral care, general administrative oversight, community involvement and an essential and too frequently neglected *teaching* ministry.

(Who, but the preacher, is the logical person to train teachers and guide the wonders of Christian nurture in the local church? The clergy are those who have received professional training. They have submitted to the disciplines of continuing education. They have developed—or should have developed—the holy habits of meditation, reflection, and hard-headed study. Administrative tasks can be delegated, as can many pastoral duties, but one of the highest callings of the ministry is to *teach* the Word. Our Lord was called "rabbi." When we fail to teach the people, we are derelict. Our teaching and preaching ministries should be carefully, painstakingly coordinated. . . . There, that's enough of that parenthetical editorial. Now, back to the preparation of the sermon.)

Let me suggest that you map out your preaching program well in advance. Build it around the church year. Do you know what you will be preaching through the autumn, back-to-school, program-building weeks of Kingdomtide? What of Advent? Christmastide? Lent? (I always approach Lent with the eagerness of a fresh convert returning to the vital center of a historic faith.) Pentecost? Contrary to the counsel of classic homiliticians like Andrew Blackwood you may not want to plan a full year ahead. Yet, summer months and vacation times can be used profitably in whatever sort of advance preparation you make. R. Benjamin Garrison, whose splendid content and remarkable literary style make him one of the most effective Protestant communicators today, uses his summer vacation in the isolated northwoods of Wisconsin as the place of beginning for the pulpit fare that will be delivered from one of the most strategic university pulpits in the land. He fishes, enjoys his family and ignores his telephone while there. He also reads, writes, and ruminates.

Take a block of time and use it for planning and for preparation. Perhaps you will be preaching a series of sermons on prayer (Alexander Whyte, the great Scottish divine, preached twice each Sunday for a full year on the text: "Lord, teach us to pray. . . ."), or on the Holy Spirit, on world hunger or the Ten Commandments or the Native American or economic avarice, or some specific ingredients of a timeless gospel. Consult reviews and bibliographies. Determine what you *ought* to be reading —then read and read and read with pen and notebook in hand, with phrases boldly underlined and margins cluttered with personal comments and reactions.

When you plan ahead prepare folders for your use. Put the name or the theme of the proposed sermon on each folder. Then, when ideas come, when you read a pertinent article, when you stumble over a relevant quotation, drop it in the appropriate folder. Build up for future use. This can be done matter-of-factly, without a great deal of self-conscious fanfare or production, until it becomes an almost unconscious by-product of broad study and general reading.

How then is a particular sermon for a particular week to be forged? Why not pen a quick, comprehensive, suggestive outline on Monday? Let it simmer, fill in its details on Thursday and write it in full on Friday or Saturday morning. No rule of thumb can be enforced. To each his own. Yet, the kind of in-depth study that precedes such preparation economizes the time and energy investment when writing a particular sermon and safeguards other days and hours for equally important tasks in present day ministry.

I'm afraid these suggestions have seemed mechanical. To a degree they are. Sermon preparation, week after week, requires a well-ordered mind. But, beyond the organization, beyond the mechanics—there must be a vital chemistry at work.

The basic chemistry of sermon preparation—and this I have already suggested—results from a continuing interaction with people.

Robert Raines in his book, *The Secular Congregation*, described the difference between a church in Independence, Iowa, in 1900 and a church in Germantown, Pennsylvania, more than half a century later. The people who gathered in that Independence congregation "knew each other, for better or worse, intimately. Every day of the week they worked, talked, fought, played, loved and hated together—learning to live a corporate life of permanent stability." Their church reflected the commonality of their life together. (Incidentally, there are countless churches in small-town America—remember, for eight years I have served my church in the Dakotas—that haven't changed that much over the past seventy-five years. They remain more like Independence than Germantown.) But, there are other churches in communities like Germantown. We know them too. The people live lives of constant mobility. They come to worship anonymously, as isolated individuals. "They come," Raines says, "not as a family but a lonely crowd. The biblical word falls on ground that has not been corporately plowed. The sermon is given the impossible burden of trying to re-create a covenant community which is not even in existence."

How, then, given the mobility, the anonymity, the uncertainty of the contemporary scene, can that "covenant community" be built? In the Germantown church Bob Raines talked about it in terms of a new and demanding kind of membership preparation. There were seminars and koinonia groups for the new members. There were the "task-oriented mission groups"; the Glass Door (a kind of teen-ager hangout, tutoring and employment center), Wellsprings (an ecumenical action group dedicated to the renewal of metropolitan Philadelphia), the Mental Health Mission Group and Covenant House. And there were study groups—groups that followed the lectionary in Bible study and that studied modern artists, dramatists, and novelists. These many in-search and outreach programs brought vital sections of the congregation together in the warm and intimate ties of thought and personhood shared. Thus, the worship experience was the outgrowth of the total life of the people; the celebration of their sense of community.

We had much the same experience at Broadway in Indianapolis during the 1960s. Nurturing fellowship groups were meeting in the church, in homes across the parish, in offices downtown. They were studying Galatians or Amos, *The Exploding Metropolis* or *God's Colony in Man's World*, Trueblood or Bonhoeffer. Out of this group life and out of our shared tasks in mission—the Thrift Shop, the sewing and cooking clubs, the Outpost Church Schools, the Health Clinic, Well-Baby Clinic, Planned Parenthood Clinic, the tutoring program, the teen-canteen—out of our community organization and neighborhood ministries a new sense of identity emerged. So, when I preached on Sunday morning I was preaching, not to a faceless mass of strangers, but to fellow seekers and co-ministers. We had been together through the week in study and mission. Now we were together to raise our voices in song, to praise the Lord and break the Word of life. We had gone over common ground. We had developed a dialogical style, had worked through conceptual data and matters of vocabulary together. Now, *communication* was possible. The people were not an audience but a congregation. The preacher was not a star performer but a member of the body.

How do you "build" a sermon for a setting like that? It grows out of the living reality of the people. It will be informed by the authority of the Scriptures and by intensive and well-organized study. It will be informed by newspaper columns, television documentaries and by involvements in a real and demanding world of events. It will draw from poetry, art and literature, but above all else, it will respond to the life situations and historic context of *the people*. "The people," cried Carl Sandburg, "Yes, the people." Where do preachers fit into this? "What they sing is the song of the people."

This sensitivity to and interaction with persons does not necessarily lead to concession and compromise. In fact, it dare not. The sermon will be more than the distilled experience of the gathered congregation. It *will* be informed by Scripture; it *will* be informed by the pastor's study; it *will* be informed by an impatient grasp of history; it *will* be informed by chaos and crisis and dire human need.

Reinhold Niebuhr was known primarily as a Christian philosopher and ethicist, as well as a political realist. Yet, he was a preacher par excellence. Alan Paton, the distinguished South African novelist and humanitarian, recently said, "I have heard many speakers in my life, and Reinhold Niebuhr was the greatest of them all." One of Niebuhr's colleagues at Union Theological Seminary said that "from *hearing* him professors and students alike, doctors and lawyers, politicians, authors, editors, long unaccustomed to taking seriously anything that emanated from the pulpit, began to read his books and discuss his theology." What kind of sermons did he preach? They were related to persons and events, but they were not constricted by the short-sighted, self-serving inclinations of a congregation. One observer wrote, "A sermon by Dr. Niebuhr, any sermon, produces a strange effect upon the thoughtful hearer. It alternately depresses and exhilarates him. It is different from the typical . . . sermon which soothes and comforts the hearer, as the patter of gentle raindrops on the roof differs from a storm, with the wind tearing at the cornices and the trees bending and breaking under the violent assault of nature." Real preaching does not appeal to a lowest common denominator form of consensus. It is aware, painfully aware, of the human condition it addresses. It takes persons and their needs seriously and is informed, and in part shaped by them. But it soars beyond the human ingredients to proclaim the searching judgments and unsearchable love, the probing, intimate dynamics and the sweeping dimensions of the gospel of Jesus Christ.

That person who is possessed by the gospel as communication takes place is a preacher in the noblest sense of the word.

One of the old standard textbooks that instructed many of us was *On the Preparation and Delivery of Sermons* by Broadus and Weatherspoon. Its emphasis upon "delivery" is a much needed emphasis today. Many clergy manufacture brilliant sermons. Their contents are balanced, provocative, scriptural, humane; and yet, when the moment of truth comes, the occasion when the letter is to be delivered, when the Word is to be shared, the sermon flutters like a dead leaf to the ground in front of the pulpit. It has no life, no vitality. It may be delivered in dull monotone; it may be haltingly read as if by a stranger; it may be dispassionately half-heartedly tossed to the winds with a shrug. The Broadus-Weatherspoon textbook says it better than I: "Delivery does not consist merely, or even chiefly, in vocalization and gesticulation, but it implies that one is possessed with the subject . . . completely in sympathy with it and fully alive to its importance, that he (or she) is not repeating remembered words but setting free the thoughts that are shut up in [the] mind."

By a strange quirk of fate Arthur J. Moore died in Atlanta the same day Mrs. Martin Luther King, Sr., was shot to death at her beloved Ebenezer Church. I heard

TELLING TRUTH

Arthur Moore at his prime when he was a bishop of the church and I was a fledgling minister in the South. What a preacher he was! Almost entirely self-taught his faith was true to tradition, his ideas bore wings, his illustrations were moving and urgent, his vocabulary was remarkable in its range and poetic in its expression—but his delivery, his *delivery*, that's what *communicated* the truth. Sometimes his voice was gentle, sometimes thunderous, but always restrained by the discipline of self-control. He was a man aflame with his message. In an autobiography, finished when he was an old man, he wrote about his preaching. He said:

> I was literally in the grip of a passion to share Christ with my brothers and sisters everywhere; and with becoming earnestness I have tried to call our people to believe in and proclaim joyfully the good news of the gospel. Having found Christ for ourselves, we must become the captives of an inner necessity which would drive us forth to share the experience with others.

We must immerse ourselves in what and whom we are called to preach. Phillips Brooks understood, long before a man named Marshall McLuhan lived, that there is no way to divorce the medium from the message; the process from the person. William Quayle, who took his market basket to town every Monday morning to fill it with books to read said, "The sermon is the preacher up to date." He said:

> Preaching is the art of making a sermon and delivering it? Why, no, that's not preaching. Preaching is the art of making a preacher and delivering *that*. Preaching is the art of the man giving himself to the throng by means of voice

and gesture and face and brains and heart, and
the background of all these, himself. . . . Therefore, the elemental business in preaching is not
with the preaching, but with the preacher. It is
no trouble to preach, but a vast trouble to con-
struct a preacher.

The preacher, through the delivery of the sermon,
spends and shares the self. Apart from such spending and
sharing the sermon is incomplete.

Chapter Five

Chapter Five

Prophets: False and True

During the last days of the Nixon administration Rabbi Baruch M. Korff was the most zealous and faithful of the President's defenders. He formed the National Citizens' Committee for Fairness to the Presidency, met with the President, wrote a book about their conversations, visited San Clemente time and time again, hosted a Washington banquet for more than 1500 of the President's supporters, dined with cabinet members, conferred with Administration aides, and lobbied against the possible impeachment of Mr. Nixon. To suggest that his role was controversial is a gross understatement.

One rabbi friend said, "[Korff] is the most brilliant man I've ever met."

Another rabbi said, "He's a charlatan."

A former member of his congregation in New Hampshire said, "He was a good rabbi; kind, gentle, and bright."

Another former parishioner said, "He was a joker. I will say no more than that. He was false."

Korff illustrates our dilemma. Who is a faithful servant; a true prophet? And who is a "joker," a charlatan? a false prophet?

Later we will consider some guidelines, but first let me describe another rabbi, one about whom there seems to be little question. Leo Baeck was a spiritual leader of the prestigious Fasanenstrasse Synagogue in Berlin when Adolf Hitler came to power. At the peak of his intellectual and religious influence, Baeck was president of Germany's B'nai B'rith and heart of the national rabbis' association, he taught at Lehranstalt and was the most popular lecturer at the Jewish "School of Wisdom" at Darmstadt; and, he had been an adviser on Jewish affairs to the Weimar Republic. Hitler, when he seized the reigns of government, organized the Reich's Representative Council of German Jews—a public relations piece of window-dressing, designed to create the impression that the official Nazi attitude toward Jewish people was harmless and respectable. The Jews of Germany chose Leo Baeck to be president of the association. Why? One of their number answered the question:

> They chose their greatest Rabbi . . . for with that sense for the future which long suffering seems to have bred within us Jews, they felt that this time of need required a man who would not only strive to meet the archenemy with the weapons of worldly wisdom. It [had] to be a man wearing the armor the prophets wore when, in the name of a just and holy God, they called the rulers of their time to battle . . . a man who drew his full strength out of his living belief in God. . . .

When the so-called Nuremberg Laws were promulgated and Jews were officially designated second-class citizens, Baeck composed a vigorous resistance prayer and sent it to every Jewish congregation in Germany with instructions to have it read during the Rosh Hashanah services. He was seized by the Gestapo, interrogated and released. Later he would be arrested over and over again. Finally, he was sent to the concentration camp at Terezin —where he became the spiritual core of that community of the damned. He conducted illegal worship services and seminars, took charge of the camp's governing body, cared for the sick and the aged and wrote his own testament of faith, *This People Israel,* which was smuggled out of Terezin on scraps of paper. Rabbi Baeck once explained the particularity of the Jew. He wrote:

> There exists the fact that *one* people, a tiny people . . . stood at Sinai, that the task to remain true to itself was set for it . . . until the end of time. Nothing rational can explain it. The fact exists, this fact of this people as the carrier of the revelation. . . . Therefore, a Jew should be a man of reason, but completely a Jew, completely within his particularity, living completely within the tradition without which there would be no history.

That consciousness of God's holy nature and a covenant relationship, that awareness of a special religious identity and mission in history, helps distinguish the true prophet of the Lord. In times of national stress such voices are desperately needed whether we think in the biblical context of exile and captivity, or present-day reality symbolized by words like "holocaust," "Solzhenitsyn," "apartheid," "Vietnam," "Watergate" and "CIA."*

---

* For a further discussion of Rabbi Baeck, see Armstrong's, *Wilderness Voices,* Abingdon, 1974, Chapter 8.

One of the genuine tragedies of that which currently passes for Christianity is its lack of "Jewishness." We have neglected the Old Testament; many of us have eliminated it from our lectionaries. So, relying upon a distorted view of the New Covenant, our faith has become more individualistic, more self-serving, more comfort-oriented and acculturated, while the stern and righteous judgments and the sense of collective responsibility implicit in the Old Covenant have been conveniently brushed aside. We ignore the obvious. Jesus was a Jew. Paul was a Jew. Christianity, emerging from the womb of Judaism, was a child of the parent. Jesus never broke from his past. He said he had come, not to destroy, but to fulfill both the Law and the prophetic content of his heritage.

Jesus considered himself in the tradition of the prophets. It is not surprising that his disciples, when asked what people were saying about him, replied that he was thought to be John the Baptist or Elijah or Isaiah, *one of the prophets*. Nor is it surprising that he defined faithfulness in prophetic terms. "How blest you are," he said, "when you suffer insults and persecution and every kind of calumny for my sake. . . . [That is how] they persecuted the prophets before you" (Matt. 5:11, 12 NEB).

The Bible speaks of many kinds of prophets. There were the cult prophets, the professional or court prophets and the great individual prophets we have come to claim as a part of our sacred history. There were prophets false and there were prophets true. What differentiated them? How can we tell the difference today?

In a word, a false prophet is unfaithful, is disobedient; violates a sacred covenant with God. Other interests, lesser values, self-delusion keep intruding. Someone has said, "We are never so sinful as when we are religious."

Think about it. The pretensions of religion create their own tremendous responsibilities. We profane the sacred by our blasphemous inconsistencies. We blame God for *our* blind spots and exploit him by identifying him with *our* biases and lesser loyalties. We justify war by making God a partisan, nationalistic, violent God. We justify vicious social, racial and economic discrimination by saying, "God made us as we are. He is the author of the differences among us." In the light of unprecedented poverty and hunger (450 million people verge on starvation) we justify "life boat" and "triage" solutions by appealing to national interest and crassly saying, "God helps those who help themselves." The false prophet is one who succumbs to the furtive desire to put one's own interests in the center of his or her universe—in the name of religion.

The Wisdom writer of Proverbs called the false prophet a "false witness." False witnesses were "full of deceit" (Prov. 12:17); they told "pack(s) of lies" (14:5). Jeremiah was more pointed. According to the Moffatt translation, they were "windbags" (Jer. 5:13). They pandered to popular opinion and substituted wishful thinking for the Word of God (Jer. 28). They cried, " 'Peace, peace' when there was no peace" (Jer. 6:14 & 8:11).

Here hard questions need to be asked of us. We say we are called to communicate truth.

How often do we curb truth, hedge truth, cut back on the whole cloth of truth in order to make our words more palatable?

How often does our own wishful thinking, or prior commitments, our own fond hopes and fears, supplant the Word of God in our preachments?

How often do we permit the pressures of popular opinion to dictate our message?

Do you remember the Mayaguez incident? From our present vantage point we have almost forgotten it (in spite of the special report released by the General Accounting Office before the presidential election of 1976). Yet, it revealed so much about one side of our national character and the mood of the American church. On May 12, 1975, the Cambodians seized an American merchant ship in disputed waters in the Gulf of Siam. We had already been humiliated by the Vietnam War. What was needed was a show of force. So, we bypassed the United Nations, ignored customary diplomatic channels and took matters into our own hands. United States warplanes blasted five Cambodian vessels out of the water. American marines boarded the Mayaguez and invaded Koh Tang Island. Fighter bombers bombed an air base and an oil depot near Sihanoukville on the Cambodian mainland —and the sovereign soil of Thailand was used, without the consent of the Thai government, to launch the attacks. Forty-one Americans died in the action. Seventy Americans were wounded. No one seemed to know (or care) how many Cambodian soldiers and civilians were killed. All of this was done to save a crew of thirty-eight men; a crew that had been well treated by their captors; a crew that was about to be released anyway (a communication from the Cambodian Government Radio promising the release of the Mayaguez was received by the White House *before* the military assault began). But, it was a display of strength and that was considered all-important. As Henry Kissenger said at the time, the lives of the Mayaguez crew members "must unfortunately be a secondary consideration." It was more important to prove we were still the toughest kid on the block.

And the vast majority of the American people seemed genuinely elated. Forget right and wrong, we seemed to say—if only we had acted with *that* kind of decisiveness in Vietnam how different the story would have been. For the moment President Ford's popularity skyrocketed. One syndicated columnist wrote, "An elephant stepped on a gnat." And we loved it! But where was the voice of biblical judgment? of Christian conscience? You tell me. . . .

False prophets, prodded or anesthetized by public opinion, gullible in the face of "official" explanations, misrepresent the truth. They wear blinders in the presence of embarrassing reality or external pressure. They cry "peace, peace" when there is no peace, fearful that too much concern about such weighty matters as justice and righteousness will affect the in-gathering of the tithe.

In the Old Testament, *false prophets were voices for hire;* they owed their influence to entrenched power; they commercialized the Word of God. They identified with unholy kings in unholy causes (1 Kings 22), or, like Hananiah, they supported the self-serving policies of their rulers against legitimate dissent. Jeremiah cried out at him, "Listen, Hananiah. The Lord has not sent you, and you have led this nation to trust in false prophecies" (Jer. 28:15).

Here hard questions need to be asked of us.

Do we not receive salaries and special considerations? Are we not for hire? What strings are attached to those resources that make possible our ministries?

We receive favors from friends, ecclesiastical "superiors," government officials and financial interests. Do we not shape the content of our proclamation in ways to court the approval of those who are in positions to strengthen our hands and make more secure our positions?

In the summer of 1976 the *New York Times* paid unusual tribute to Bishop Paul Moore, Jr., of the diocese of

New York. He has become a catalyst; a rallying point for social change in a beleaguered city. Born to wealth he has identified, as too few church leaders have, with the poor and the powerless. He began his parish ministry in the slums of Newark. I first knew him in Indianapolis where, for six years, we stood side by side dealing with issues of community organization and civil rights in the inner city. In the nation's capitol, as suffragan bishop, he worked for home rule. Moore is no stranger to conflict. The *Times* wrote, "His campaign has not only generated wide interest but has also signalled the most important thrust of churches into the city's affairs in recent history."

What had focused the spotlight on Bishop Moore? Three prophetic sermons and numerous appearances before civic and business groups dealing with New York City's financial crisis. In "a ringing Easter sermon" he scored the exodus of corporate and industrial resources from the center-cities of the land thus narrowing their tax bases and penalizing the already impoverished. He cried, "Executives, reverse your decisions and stay in the city. Cut through the fog of statistics and see the moral decision behind them. *Be part of the rising, not the dying.*"

In a sermon to his Diocesan Convention in May he said:

> I want to say here today, clearly and strongly, that the blame for the root causes for the disintegration of New York and our other cities cannot be placed at the feet of businesses alone. Many others are to blame. Generations of government on many levels have committed New York and other cities to a devastating debt load, under which we now stagger.

He went on to include the press for failing to alert the

public, labor unions with their exhorbitant demands, academic institutions and "special interest groups of all kinds." He charged that "our churches, unused to dealing with problems of government finance, have kept their silence too long. There's enough blame to go around," he added.

On July 5, at the Cathedral of St. John the Divine, he preached a bicentennial sermon. Among other things, he said:

> I declare to you . . . that we New Yorkers *are* citizens of the USA. Old glory is *our* flag. It stands for our values of freedom, compassion, independence of spirit, pluralism.
>
> It is New York City, even in its hour of peril, that best represents the values of the land. We are not about to be sawed off and cast into the sea!
>
> For it is out of our nurseries, our schools, our universities, our settlement houses that successive waves of immigrants set forth to build America.
>
> And it is into our ghettos, our hospitals, our nursing homes that the weak and the poor of America retreat when they are cast off by our more fortunate neighbors.
>
> Therefore, let us claim our rightful place in the political and economic life of America and place on the top of our agenda the *federalization of Health, Education and Welfare cost of the poor.*

Preaching to corporate giants within his own diocese and visitors from across the land on three separate occasions (and on many others) he was a true prophet, running the risks of intense criticism, speaking on behalf of the powerless.

The false prophet is intimidated by those who pay the

bills; is silenced by their threats of economic boycott; is neutralized by prospects of disapproval.

In the epistles false prophets were seen as "false teachers." They proclaimed dangerous heresies (2 Peter 2 and 1 John 4). Jesus called them "wolves in sheep's clothing" (Matt. 7:15). One New Testament writer said, "Purdition waits for them with unsleeping eyes" (2 Pet. 2:3).

Once again, hard questions need to be asked.

Is our proclamation consistent with the living Word of God? I am not calling for a literalistic interpretation of the Bible (scholarship and common sense will not permit that); I am not asking for a naïve and exclusive acceptance of scriptural authority. But if the Bible is the source book of our faith, if it *is* the Word of God, we have no right to abandon the burden of its message in our proclamation.

Those who, a few years ago, announced the "death of God" were heretics. They had strayed far afield from the biblical revelation.

Today we hear the claims and counterclaims of special interests. The "will of God" is linked with Marxist economics, with Arab terrorism and Zionism in the Middle East, with an assortment of liberation movements and with the fulminations of such disparate characters as Fidel Castro, Ian Smith, and the Rev. Sun Myung Moon. More important, from our vantage point as North Americans, there have been those who have insisted that "what is good for General Motors is good for us." The antics of the CIA in Chile and Cuba, the so-called national interest of the "American empire" and the credos of the U.S. Chamber of Commerce and multi-national corporations have been confused with the historic fulfillment of the Christian faith. What an obscene blaspheme. Dare we put our Lord in the exclusive pocket of any single national dream, economic system, revolutionary ideal or utopian political scheme? In spite of recent revelations concerning the CIA's use of missionary personnel I assume you know the answer.

A well-known preacher, excusing himself for not criticizing his nation's foreign policy at its most vulnerable points, argues that he is a New Testament evangelist, not an Old Testament prophet. That sort of rationalization simply won't "wash." The evangelist and the prophet, the Old Testament and the New, are expressions of one, integrated gospel. To dismember that gospel and compartmentalize it is to betray the living Word. It is heresy.

A false prophet is one whose moral life is weighed and found wanting. The Bible speaks of inexcusable concessions to Baal worship and fertility rites in Canaan, of temple prostitution and dissolute practices and greed for money. If ours is, as we say, an incarnational faith, then the life we live cannot be divorced from the message we preach.

There are more hard questions to be asked. Am I the person I pretend to be? Am I honest with myself and others? Do the most intimate relationships of my life reflect compassion, understanding, and profound respect for the personhood of the people involved? Do I use people to obtain my objectives? Are my priorities more centered in things I can accumulate, power I can acheive, persons I can exploit or are they the servants of people I can genuinely share my life with and causes I am called to serve?

We are products of our pasts. Religiously, our approaches to morality have been shaped by the Ten Commandments, nineteenth-century revivalism and threads of perfectionism running through many of our traditions. My grandfather, when a young preacher in the Northwest Territory, wrote a widely read article "proving," beyond any doubt, that card-playing, taking the Lord's name in vain, smoking, drinking alcoholic beverages, theatre-going and dancing were of the devil. "Holiness" consisted of abstaining from the above, praying, attending church and "doing good" (although the deeds were nowhere spelled out and motives were not explored). I mention this only because it was altogether typical and, therefore, joins my personal history with that of many of the readers of these words. Our parents saw sin as "the willful transgression on the known law"—narrowly defined. The Sermon on the Mount was viewed as an impossible dream or an "interim ethic" rather than a statement on present moral responsibility.

Culturally, Puritan and Victorian influences, as reflected in Hawthorne's *Scarlet Letter*, and Arthur Miller's *The Crucible* reinforced the rigidity, the hypocrisy and the sexual preoccupation of religious tradition.

Washington has aided and abetted the narrow confines of customary moral evaluation. Watergate was succeeded by a series of lurid sex scandals in the nation's capitol. Suddenly the American public was deluged with "background data" on Washington, Jefferson, Jackson, Cleveland, Harding, Roosevelt, Eisenhower and Kennedy, suggesting that there was nothing new under the sun. In the religious worlds, skeletons were dragged from the closets of Henry Ward Beecher and Bishop James Cannon. These were joined by exposés related to such divergent characters as Paul Tillich, Martin Luther King, Jr., Billy James Hargis, and Bishop James Pike. Long ago Martin Luther had to face his accusers (a nun's place was *not* in the home) and John Wesley's wife endured her tragic marriage.

The Ten Commandments have not been rescinded, and

permissiveness, moral relativity and situation ethics admittedly have been used to rationalize a multitude of sins. But, the message we preach has at its very center a doctrine of forgiveness. It does not seek to deny the universality of sin, the grace of compassion and acceptance and the reality of redeeming love in human/divine relationships. Michael Novak, in a perceptive if somewhat overstated article during the height of the Washington sex scandals, suggested that "Purity is not a fitting national goal—it is not nearly so important as justice or wisdom." With tongue in cheek he added, "Why should we discriminate against cads and rakes? They may compose the single best source of supply of decent, just, practical and wise politicians—not to mention journalists. And after Paul Tillich, it may be said, theologians." Acknowledging the exceeding sinfulness of sin, I for one, am grateful for "immoral" men like Thomas Jefferson, Henry Ward Beecher, Franklin Roosevelt, and Paul Tillich (not to mention King David) enriching our common experience and helping us better understand some of the higher meanings of justice and righteousness. True biblical holiness is broader and more basic than our narrow views have argued.

Phillips Brooks once said, "The truth must come. . . . through the person, not merely over his lips, not merely into his understanding and through his pen. It must come through his character, his affections, his whole intellectual and moral being." That is true, and morality, properly conceived, deals with the ultimacy of other-centered love in every conceivable situation. When love is betrayed, when persons are used and dehumanized, when sacred covenants are violated, when justice is denied and righteousness perverted, then the plumb line is telling in its judgments. A false prophet is one whose pretensions and loyalties deny the truth proclaimed.

A false prophet can be extremely convincing. *Jesus warned about those who would offer "many signs and wonders" as their credentials* (Mark 13:22). The false prophet can offer ecstatic utterances and often performs deeds that appear magic—but the ministry is a false, misleading ministry. "Many false prophets will arise and will mislead many," said the son of Man (Matt. 24:11).

False prophets tend to pamper themselves; do what they do for the sake of themselves. They may promise gifts of healing and tongues and miracles, special powers, appealing to the selfish instincts of believers. Jesus was tempted to cultivate this sort of ministry. "Throw yourself from the parapet of the temple," the evil one said. "Tell these stones to become bread." "Fall down and do me homage," said the tempter, "and the kingdoms of the world are yours" (Matthew 4:1–10). "Begone Satan," said our Lord, as he kept his values and priorities intact.

The so-called charismatic movement is a current phenomena, but when divorced from the risk-taking and sacrifice a vital faith requires, it becomes a self-serving exercise. There must be no forced choice between a personal faith and its social application. When asked to choose up sides in the Hartford Statement/Boston Statement/Chicago Declaration controversey some time ago, an Episcopalian said, "It's like asking which leg do you most need to walk with. You need both transcendence and immanence, both spirituality and social action."

Once again, there are hard questions that need to be asked of us.

Do we tend to transfer selfishness to the realm of the spirit?

Do we promise gifts and graces, in the name of religious faith, that have little significance beyond what they can do for the recipient? to make that person feel good? happy? enjoy the headiness of special powers?

Do we turn our verbalization of the gospel into blasphemy by not incarnating the humility, unselfishness and sacrifice implicit in the song that says, "the way of the cross leads home."

It is one thing to seek, embrace and express genuine gifts of the Spirit. It is quite another thing to huckster those gifts for the sake of personal power and ego-satisfaction.

Perhaps I have given too much time and attention to "false prophets." But, I don't think so. Knowing my own temptations and inclinations, I don't think so.

Now—*What about authentic prophetic ministry? How can we determine its authenticity? What are its characteristics and guidelines?*

The prophets of the Lord grounded their message in the Word of the Lord, a Word that reflected and demonstrated the very nature of God. The absolute, infinite righteousness of God provided the authority for prophetic utterance. Amos, Isaiah and the others found in the ineffable holiness of God "the hinge on which all history swings." You see, it is the *character* of God that gives power to his Word. Jeremiah said the divine Word is like a hammer that breaks rocks to pieces (Jer. 23:29); in the prophet's mouth it becomes a fire that devours people like wood (Jer. 5:14). Isaiah said it lights upon Israel and the entire nation reels under its impact (Isa. 9:7, 8). It hews like a sword, cried Hosea (6:5); and Amos, the incomparable, insisted that when God Almighty lifts his voice and roars, the pastures and the forests of Carmel wither (Amos 1:2); an unfaithful land cannot bear, cannot endure, the searching implications of his Word (Amos 7:10).

True prophecy is rooted in the God of that Word and in the continuing, living Word of God.

God entered into a covenant with his people. It was not a covenant of equals, but was sealed by the "lord of lords," "the kings of kings," by Yahweh, the Almighty. The covenant was first forged at Sinai, but it is an ongoing covenant that each new generation must accept as its own. The voice of Deuteronomic reform said:

> The Lord our God made a covenant with us at Horeb. Not with our fathers did the Lord make this covenant, but with us, who are all of us here alive this day (Deut. 5:2, 3).

We cannot inherit the blessedness of a covenant relationship. Each generation must renew its loyalty. Isaac had to redig the wells his father had first dug. So too must we if ministry is to be authentic.

When a people violate their covenant with God, disobey his claims and turn away from his righteousness they come under judgment. True. Yet, these are only religious words unless fleshed out with particular charges and specific judgments. Nor is God the God alone of those who acknowledge his sovereignty. He is the God of every person, every nation, everywhere. Thus the prophets cried against specific deeds and practices, specific attitudes and policies, against the unrighteousness of both their own people and of others.

Damascus had battered Gilead with "iron-studded sledges" (Amos 1:3) thus violating the law of proportionality in warfare.

Ammon had "ripped up pregnant women in Gilead" (Amos 1:13), had pushed out its nation's borders on the basis of war crimes and atrocities.

Moab burned the bones of defected kings (Amos 2:1). Tyre and Gaza carried their enemies off into slavery (Amos 1:6, 9).

Edom—reflecting the instincts of so many of us— "pursued his brother with a sword in his hand . . . stifled compassion, nursed the anger in his heart, and cherished his fury" (Amos 1:11).

But the objects of the prophet's scorn were not just Damascus, Gaza, Tyre, Edom, Ammon and Moab, Canaan and Babylon—Stalin's Russia, Mao's China, Castro's Cuba, Amin's Uganda and southern Africa; ungodly nations "out there" somewhere. The prophets zeroed in on their own favored land.

The wealthy trampled on the heads of the poor and callously neglected the underprivileged in Israel (Amos 2:7).

The "cows of Bashan," the "playgirls" of that ancient world, wallowing in their new found wealth, "oppressed the weak and crushed the needy" in Judah (Amos 4:1).

"Like a wild heifer Israel is wild," cried Hosea (Hos. 4:16).

The Nazarites broke their vows and became drunkards, priests committed murder and permitted temple prostitution, judges accepted bribes and oppressed the innocent, princes were corrupt, false prophets beat their drums and beguiled the susceptible—Israel had become as a "silly dove . . . without sense" (Hos. 7:11).

So Judah and Israel, having violated the covenant, were under special judgment—and the prophets said so. Sometimes these prophets were banished, as was Amos; sometimes humiliated and imprisoned, as was Jeremiah—but they remained true to the Word of God. They refused to substitute aesthetics and elaborate ritual, social acceptability and civil religion, for justice and honor.

"I hate, I spurn your feasts," cried the dresser of sycamores, "I take no pleasure in your festal gathering . . . Take away from me the noise of your songs. . . . Let justice roll down like waters, and righteousness as a mighty stream" (Amos 5:21, 23, 24).

What has this to do with us as we consider the communication of truth in a difficult time? Just about everything!

Moses, the first of the authentic prophets, stood before a head of state, identified with the oppressed of his day, and said, "Let my people go." Prophetic voices are echoing that plea around the world today.

I have met and talked with Raul Cardinal Silva Henriquez twice; once in 1972, once in 1976. In 1972 Cardinal Silva was walking a tightrope. Salvador Allende, a radical socialist, was president of Chile. Cardinal Silva was not a Marxist and was impatient with some of his young priests who confused a utopian economic system and an idyllic philosophy of history with gospel imperatives. But, he was committed to the constitutionality of Allende's government and to the validity of many of his reforms. In 1976 the military junta was in control and the tightrope was more precarious. Power had been seized. Allende had been murdered. The constitution had been abrogated. Human rights, as defined by the United Nations, had been radically violated. Political prisoners were tortured. Those whose views ran counter to the junta, no matter how moderate, were either arrested, deported or put in jeopardy. Economic policies that led to inflation and large scale unemployment shifted the burdens to the poor. Cardinal Silva said, "The Church must be the voice of all, especially of those who do not have a voice." The cardinal, by the nature of his heroic witness, risks his security and physical well-being each day of his life.

True prophecy, however, is not limited to "princes" of the church (in fact, it is seldom found among powerful administrators and decision makers). Nearly thirty years ago an ugly, stooped, quite ordinary Albanian nun walked away from the Sisters of Loreto convent for affluent girls in Darjeeling, donned a white and blue sari, and offered herself to the most destitute of the world. Mother Teresa went to Calcutta to become one with the starving.

Dom Helder Camara, one of the few Christians on the present scene who might upstage Mother Teresa, stopped midway through a speech at a Eucharistic Congress, walked to the bent-over little woman, bowed and kissed both of her hands—"in the name of the poor of all the world." Mother Teresa has said, "To help us go to heaven Christ made one condition. . . . When we come before him, we will be judged by what we have been to the poor."

Nor is true prophecy the special province of professional religionists. Fred Morris, a young American businessman in Brazil (who had once been a missionary), was arrested by military police in that country on September 30, 1974. Held for seventeen days, he was tortured by the police and brutally interrogated because of his friendship with Dom Helder. In a moving article in the *Christian Century* he described the faith that sustained him. He wrote:

> Perhaps more important than anything else for me personally—after ten years of seeking to identify with the people of Brazil, whom I have come to love so much, I was compelled to participate in their suffering. . . . I was suffering at

the hands of the same oppressor that oppresses them. For that period, at least, the privilege of being a part of the Brazilian people was forced upon me. I shared in the communion of those saints.

What has all of this to do with preaching to middle American congregations? Surely you understand the implications. Unless the local church can somehow, through its lay and clerical leadership, identify with the pathos and drama of Third and Fourth World suffering, poverty and powerlessness, we will continue in an insulated realm of self-protective irrelevance.

John Adams, an Air Force pilot and POW in World War II, has long been a close friend of mine. More recently he has become something of a hero. Representing the Church of Jesus Christ he has worked with the U.S. Justice Department, and with a variety of liberation and "movement" groups during the Poor Peoples' March, at the political conventions of '72 and '76, at Kent State and Jackson State, at Wounded Knee, and, more recently, in a reopening of the Robert Spike murder case and the criminal excesses of the FBI. In a recent book, *At the Heart of the Whirlwind,* he says, "After having pastored churches for more than fifteen years, I discovered that a pastoral role could be performed in the midst of social conflict." Describing his ministry of crisis intervention he writes:

Just as in a local church congregation this ministry called for interpreting the gospel, seeking the guidance of the Holy Spirit, developing trust, sharing moral insights and retaining confidences. . . . [It] involved social presence rather than social activism.

"Just as in the local congregation. . . ." There you have it. Unless the local congregation is truly prophetic, both in presence and in action, the church is immobilized. As Adams insists, the pastoral role dare not be minimized (see chapter 6), but anything less than prophetic witness is sub-Christian. And the pulpit must reflect this fundamental truth.

Prophets are alive today, as in ancient Israel. The plumb line they use is not the "will of the people" but the Word of God. Just as prophets of old were "the storm patrols of Israel's history," so today true prophetic ministry continues. As a Christian, the prophet will reflect more the compassion of Hosea than the vindictive harshness of Amos, but the judgment will be there—a judgment based on the universal application of God's love. The king, Ahab, asked the prophet, Elijah, "Art thou he that troubles Israel?" The prophet is a troublesome figure in the ongoing story of the faith. But, true prophets there must be —and, under God, there will be—if we strive to learn, preach and live the truth.

Chapter Six

Chapter Six

Truth in Love

Robert Heilbroner, who catalogued the cultural and economic diseases of the present hour in his *Inquiry into the Human Prospect,* argued that the symbols of our affluence—"higher incomes, better diets, miracles of medicine, triumphs of applied physics and chemistry"—have failed "to satisfy the human spirit." Two academicians, writing in *Psychology Today,* charged that churches are losing influence in the formation of social policy and that many people are losing interest in religion. Even so, they continued, "People still seek answers to the great questions that human beings have addressed themselves to for centuries, and they still ache to believe that someone is minding the store, that there is something beyond our personal and collective reach." There is no honest way to deny the reality of the world Heilbroner describes, a world of insane violence, economic injustice, international anarchy and moral irresponsibility. Neither is it possible to deny the fond aspirations of the human spirit. It is the function of the Christian pulpit to address both worlds, judging and seeking to redirect culture in the light of the "truth-claims" of the biblical revelation, while, at the same time, ministering to and providing nurture for the human spirit. As the writer of the Ephesian letter reminded his readers, we are called to "speak the truth in love" (Eph. 4:15).

An unusually gifted preacher, after many years of outspoken, courageous, strife-torn leadership in a distinguished pulpit, was asked by his congregation to give up his post. In conversations with friends he argued that he had been forced out because of the "stands" he had taken on controversial issues. His had been a "prophetic" ministry, he reasoned, and his people could not tolerate the hard truths of such a ministry. Those who knew the man and church thought they knew better.

One day I encountered a wealthy executive who had left the church during the man's ministry. Why had he left? "Dr. Smith never sought us out," he said. "He knew of our differences and our displeasure, but he refused to take the time to enter into conversation with us. He 'knew' he was right and that was all that seemed to matter to him."

As we talked further it became apparent that the minister's immediate predecessor, widely known for his prophetic courage, had been considered a close friend by the executive. "We didn't agree, but that made little difference," he explained. And then, with a futile shrug, he made his most telling point. "Dr. Smith just didn't seem to care." The Christian ministry can suffer no more damning an indictment: "He 'knew' he was right. . . . He didn't seem to care."

The Messiah of the Christian faith *cared*. Too often

those who minister in his name seem to disregard the feelings and convictions of others as they bulldoze, full steam ahead, toward their self-determined goals. Jesus moved toward clearly defined destinations, but he always had time for people on the way. His goals were under constant attack and his path was often blocked by those who took sharp issue with him. So he paused, dealt with his questioners, reasoned with his critics, and then continued on. He always seemed to have time to enter into thoughtful exchanges with those who were threatened by his ministry. Sometimes they heeded his words and their lives were changed forever. Sometimes they taunted and rejected him. But they were never ignored.

Jesus was not spineless in the presence of hostility; far from it, he met it with confidence and grace. He did not recant or retreat when challenged by those who disagreed. But he had time for them, saw their potential, respected and tried to persuade them. He spoke the truth in love. When some of us are challenged we sulk or shout, moodily lick our wounds and steal away, avoiding that confrontation that could prove to be redemptive. What a contrast to Jesus who, as he hung on a crude Roman gibbet, offered words of compassion and forgiveness to his murderers.

Whatever else we say about it, our Lord's ministry was person-centered. Oh, it was cause-oriented. He had come to announce and initiate a kingdom. But, even that kingdom was centered in persons—in little children, grasping tax collectors, grief-stricken mourners, broken women, businessmen and politicians, people who drank too much and married too often, in fishermen and widows and wealthy princes. No matter how eloquent or urgent our preaching, if the Nazarene is our model, we will begin with the people—friend and foe alike.

We have said from the outset that persons are at the

center of authentic ministry. The preacher is a human being interacting with other human beings. We begin, as all true servanthood must, with the people. "We sing the song of the people."

My father, a minister who died when much too young, was warmhearted; volatile; lovable; one of the most remarkable men I have ever known. Years ago he taught me the most dramatic pastoral lesson of my life. I was a college student. We were walking through a park in a desert town in southern California. A woman—I barely noticed her—approached us from the other direction. As she passed Dad left me, touched her arm and said, "You're in trouble. Can I help?" The woman slumped to a nearby bench and began to sob. She and her husband, travelers from a distant state, had been driving through a nearby mountain pass. A boy had darted from behind a rock. Their car had struck and killed him. The woman's husband was with the parents of the boy at that moment. And she was alone, terribly alone, in an alien, dirty desert town. What had my father seen? How had he known? What instincts had he cultivated across the years that made him that sensitive to the desperation of another?

The haunting fact is—we are surrounded by people who need the understanding and grace God can manifest through us. Social conscience is not the antithesis of pastoral concern. A girl dies a tragic death. Her brother commits suicide. Are we to withhold compassionate ministry from their parents because they are wealthy, irresponsible "jet setters"? I happen to believe George Wallace is an opportunist who built his political base on the foundations of race prejudice and has parlayed the fears and anxieties of the ignorant and misinformed on his personal ambitions for the future (ambitions that now seem forever doomed). But when his first wife died I wrote

him a letter of sympathy and, after he had been shot by
a would-be assassin, visited him in his executive offices in
Montgomery and talked and prayed with him. These
were not hypocritical gestures, but expressions of Christian concern. When I first decided to enter the ministry
an older friend, a man of relative wealth and reactionary
politics, wrote me an encouraging note and said, "Prepare
yourself as best you can. Remember, the up-and-in need
help as well as the down-and-out." Dom Helder Camara,
one of the genuine Christian heroes of our time, introduc-
ing himself to the people of Recife in 1964, asked:

> Who am I? . . . A human being who regards
> himself as a brother in weakness and sin to all
> men, of all races and creeds in the world. . . .
> A bishop of the Catholic Church who comes, in
> the imitation of Christ, not to be served but to
> serve. . . . Let no one be alarmed to see me in
> the company of men who are supposedly com-
> promising or dangerous, men in power or in the
> opposition, reformists or anti-reformists, revolu-
> tionaries or anti-revolutionaries, men of good
> faith or bad. . . . My door and my heart will be
> open to all, absolutely to all. Christ died for all.

There are hurt and pain everywhere about us. Our
preaching dare not be oblivious to that fact. Phillips
Brooks may have been a preacher preeminent, but he was
a pastor first. He wrote:

> You go to some crushed and broken heart; you
> tell what truth you know, the truth of the ever
> ready and inexhaustible forgiveness, the truth
> of the unutterable love, the truth of the un-
> broken life of immortality; and you let the sor-
> row for that heart's sorrow which you truly feel
> utter itself in whatever true and simple ways
> it will.

But, pastoral love must never be confused with irresponsible sentimentalism or a sanctimonious cloak to be worn justifying collaboration and compromise with evil.

The indomitable Ernest Fremont Tittle was one of the twentieth century's most effective and influential preachers. For more than thirty years he served a wealthy, conservative congregation in Evanston, Illinois. He was a Christian socialist surrounded by pillars of capitalism. He was a civil libertarian in a community dominated by the American Legion and Colonel McCormack's *Chicago Tribune*. He was a pacifist through all the days of World War II. And he survived, his influence unabated, until his untimely death in 1949. How was it possible in such a church in such a time? As one friend put it, "It was . . . love that made him a fighter." An ardent admirer, a Standard Oil executive, said, "Ernest Tittle is the strongest man I have known." But Tittle himself provided the underlying answer. He once wrote, "No man can preach effectively unless he knows the human heart, and no man can know the human heart unless he keeps in close touch with human lives." There you have it. To know and love people authenticates prophetic ministry. If we have not love we are nothing (1 Cor. 13:2b).

My ministry has been flawed and imperfect, far from Christlike in so many ways. It has been viewed by some as opinionated and insensitive. And it has been stormy. An editorial in a church periodical once referred to me as "one who appears to be followed by controversy wherever he goes." But I believe I have honestly tried, in the midst of stress and conflict, to reflect responsible love.

For more than eight years I have served as a United Methodist bishop in the Dakotas. During those years I have fought for the life of a young Native American sentenced to death for a brutal murder, have visited Vietnam and vigorously opposed that war, have actively supported a man I believe to be one of the most honorable men in public life, Senator George McGovern, and have served as a mediator during the siege of Wounded Knee on the Pine Ridge Reservation in 1973. I have appeared before legislative committees and press conferences in state capitols and in Washington opposing capital punishment, condemning the Thieu-Ky regime in Saigon, pleading for handgun control, supporting the recommendations of the Rome Food Conference of 1974, opposing a constitutional amendment that would prohibit abortion, and urging reconstruction aid for a devastated reunited Vietnam. These are forms of witness that have taxed the patience of many good and faithful "constituents." Never presuming to speak *for* them or the church, always stressing my role as a private citizen or as president of my denomination's Board of Church and Society, I have nonetheless embarrassed and angered persons whose worth and friendship I value far more than they know.

In the fall of 1974, during the heat of a senatorial race in South Dakota (while my wife and I were attending a peace conference in Belgium) a group of concerned members of the largest church in the Dakotas Area met and passed a resolution criticizing my "participation in political and other secular affairs outside the normal pattern of church behavior." They protested my actions and asked that I "refrain from any further activities of this nature and . . . give my time . . . and talents to the ministry of the gospel."

When we returned from Europe I counseled with a number of persons and issued a statement. Among other things I said:

When I visit Vietnam or represent a church

> agency at Wounded Knee or appear before a
> Senate sub-committee or support a particular
> candidate for public office, I do so on the basis
> of deep ethical and religious conviction, not
> because of a desire to stray from my Christian
> vocation. I try not to separate my world into
> neat compartments, drawing false distinctions
> between the "secular" and the "sacred." . . .
> [My] church is a free church. The United States
> of America is a free country. I cherish that free-
> dom and will continue to express it as prayer-
> fully and responsibly as I know how.

But to sit behind a desk and write such a statement (or to
stand behind a pulpit and deliver such a preachment) is
not enough. People who disagreed were angry and hurt-
ing. I was their pastor. So I arranged to go to the church,
meet with any and all who chose to come, listen to their
concerns and arguments, answer their questions, interpret
my actions in the light of my faith, and absorb whatever
hostility and punishment were necessary.

For two solid hours (they seemed like weeks) I stood
before more than 700 people listening and responding,
attempting to be patient and reasonable, painfully aware
of their concern and distressed by the intensity of their
feelings. There were many who were prayerfully sup-
portive, but they wisely kept their silence. The actions had
been mine; the responses needed to come from me. The
next day the local newspaper, in a three-column spread,
said: "Spirit of Reconciliation Emerges From Meeting of
Bishop Armstrong, Methodist Church Critics." It goes
without saying that all wounds were not healed, but a
necessary corner had been turned.

I have detailed the above only to say that we must
live with the consequences of our ministries. When we
seek to make a difference in a real world we will offend
and alienate good people. Responsible leadership has no

right to fire its salvoes and then beat a hasty retreat, insulating itself from inevitable (and sometimes legitimate) negative reaction. We must be pastoral. We must be willing to go to our critics, reason with them in humility, admit our mistakes, disagree with them while respecting (or at least trying to understand) their points of view— and reflect a spirit of acceptance and Christian love all the while. Under God we have no right to speak the prophetic word, representing those values and commitments we believe to be essential, unless we are willing to extend to our antagonists the grace and love our Lord provides through the ministry of his Spirit. A sensitive and open response to criticism, a genuine smile in the face of a snarl, is not a sign of weakness, it is an expression of personal security and strength.

The context of our shared ministry is confusing and demanding. The stakes—human survival, peace with justice, racial equality, personal and spiritual fulfillment— have never been higher. There are sharp divisions among and within us. Again we ask the question: What is the role of preaching in all this? Is it mortal folly? No! It is God's "foolishness." It is the covenantal act that provides celebration amidst bewilderment, inspiration amidst disenchantment and brokenness, guidance for the seeking and the waylost, and a sense of solidarity for God's people in a very human world. Such preaching, dependent upon the Spirit of God for its authority, will draw from us the best of our resources and disciplines. It must blend the pastoral with the prophetic. We are called to speak the truth in love—for truth without love is not truth.

As I suggested at the outset, the stimulus for much of this book comes from the life and ministry of Phillips Brooks. It only seems fitting that he should have the last word:

The preacher needs to be a pastor, that he may preach to real (persons). The pastor must be preacher, that he may keep the dignity of his work alive. The preacher who is not a pastor grows remote. The pastor who is not a preacher grows petty. . . . Be both, for you cannot really be one unless you also are the other.